SAVING THE OCEANS

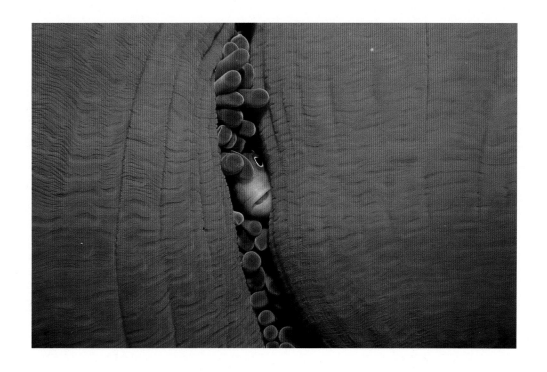

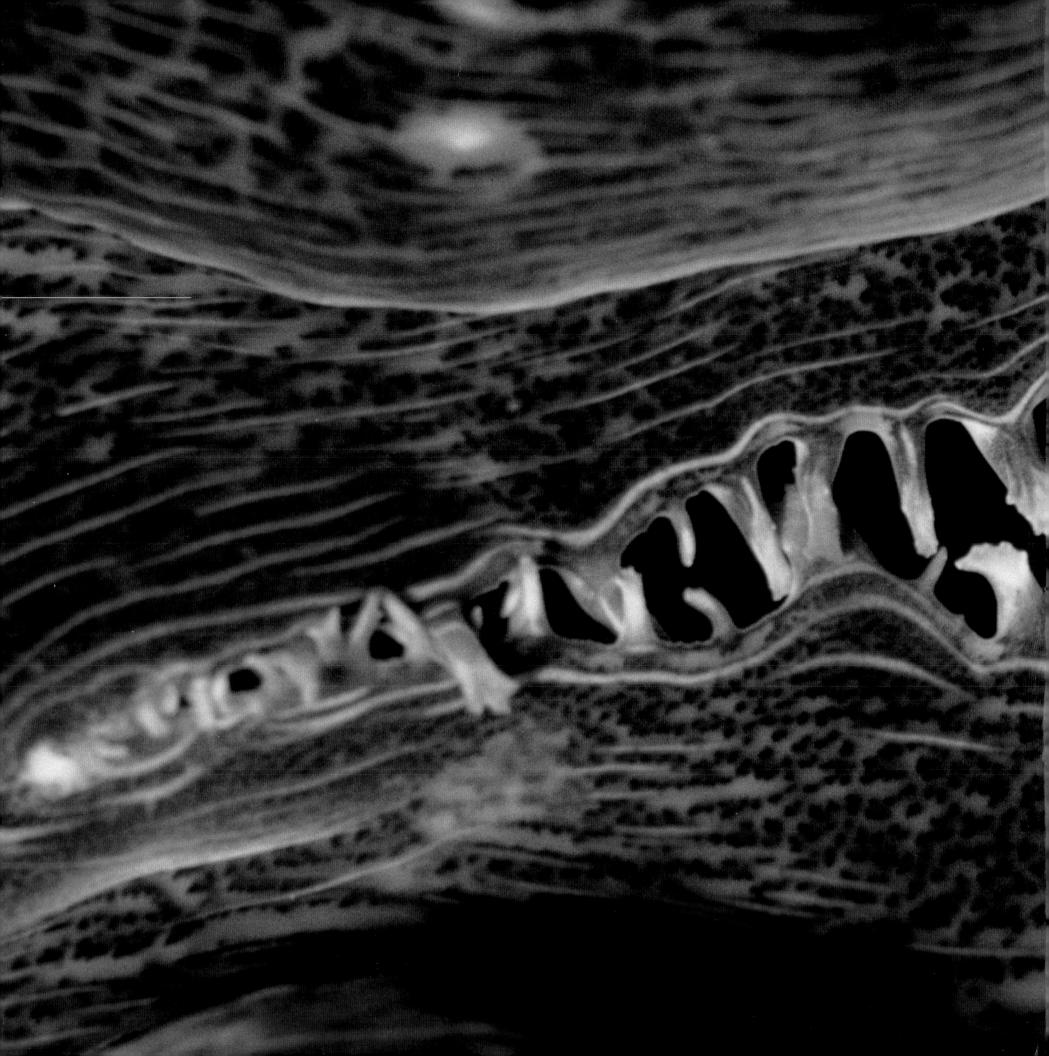

SAVING THE OCEANS

GENERAL EDITOR

JOSEPH MacINNIS

CONTRIBUTORS

MICHAEL DONOGHUE

SYLVIA EARLE

HILLARY HAUSER

JOHN LYTHGOE

RONALD ORENSTEIN

T.R. PARSONS

PETER A. RONA

ANATOLY SAGALEVITCH

MARIE THARP

FIREFLY BOOKS

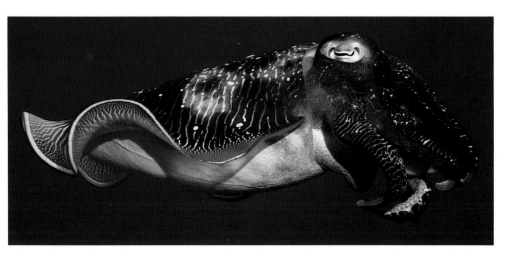

This curious-looking cuttlefish (Sepia sp.) is a relative of the squid and octopus (order Sepioidea). CARL ROESSLER

Page 1:

The sea anemone's (order Actiniaria) tentacles provide protection for this clownfish (Amphiprion). MICHELE HALL

Pages 2-3:

A closeup of the mantle of a giant clam (family Tridacnidae). CHRIS NEWBERT/SUPERSTOCK

Page 4:

Red Sea coral reef.

© DAVID DOUBILET

Pages 8-9:

A giant green sea anemone (Anthopleura xanthogrammica). JEFF FOOTT

A FIREFLY BOOK

Copyright © 1992 by Key Porter Books

Cataloguing in Publication Data

Main entry under title:

Saving the oceans

Includes index.

ISBN 1-55209-076-0

1. Marine resources conservation.
2. Marine ecology. I. Donoghue, Michael. II. MacInnis, Joe, 1937– .

GC1018.S28 1996   333.91′64
C96-930631-8

Firefly Books Ltd.,
3680 Victoria Park Avenue
Willowdale, Ontario M2H 3K1

Firefly Books (U.S.) Inc.,
P.O. Box 1338, Ellicot Station
Buffalo, New York 14205

96 97 98 99 6 5 4 3 2 1

The publisher would like to thank the following people and organizations for their assistance in the preparation of this book: J. Dick, D. Calder, and R. Winterbottom of the Royal Ontario Museum, B. Campbell of the Canadian Wildlife Service, S. Lieberman of the U.S. Fish and Wildlife Service, D. McAllister of Ocean Voice International, the International Council for Bird Preservation, and M.B. Fenton, J. Lien and D. Scott.

Marie Tharp would like to thank her staff—Deborah Bartolotta, James Doller, Lex Reibestein and Marian Doller—for their contributions to her chapter.

The chapter "The Dynamic Abyss" by Peter A. Rona was not written in his official capacity as a U.S. government employee, and does not reflect opinions of the U.S. Department of Commerce.

Design: Tania Craan and Scott Richardson
Illustrations: Dorothy Siemens
Typesetting: Compeer Typographic Services
Printed and bound in Hong Kong

CONTENTS

INTRODUCTION

JOSEPH MacINNIS

THERE ARE THREE OF US INSIDE THE SUBMERSIBLE, WHICH IS AS hot as an airtight stove. We have just left the sun-washed deck of our mother ship and are being slowly lifted over the side and into the ocean. Anatoly Sagalevitch, our Russian pilot, is stripped to the waist, his hands reaching out to the control panels, his mind running over the final pre-dive checklist: life-support systems, sub-to-surface communications, obstacle-avoidance sonar, and battery power. As he works, preparing for the 13,000-foot (4,000-m) descent, I glance out my viewport at the deep blue sea coming up at us.

The moving skin of the ocean is riffled and taut, like pulverized lapis. We are in mid-launch, 18 tons of submersible, swinging on the end of a colossal, articulating crane. As we are lowered, we begin to relinquish the rhythm of the ship and acquire the rhythm of the sea. An indigo wave, larger than the rest, rolls under us, almost touching the viewport. Quivering on its crest is an iridescent slick—hydraulic oil has leaked from the ship.

The slick is a reminder, telling me that the ocean I love is under attack, and even we who claim to be its closest friends are sometimes part of the problem.

The suffocation and death of the great waters—and the animals and plants that live within them—is taking place, around the world, every day. There are times when the mortality is so shocking it explodes into headlines. The grounding of the *Exxon Valdez*. The willful destruction of the Persian Gulf by an Iraqi psychopath. Sadly, however, most of the damage is done on a

Opposite:

Once an abundant species, the green turtle (Chelonia mydas) *is now endangered due to overhunting and degradation of its nesting and feeding habitats.*

11

The launch of the Mir 1
submersible.

much smaller scale by nice, unthinking people trying to sustain their version of economic growth.

Somewhere, in the long historical migration from *Homo habilis* kneeling at the river's edge in Africa, we lost our place within Nature. We divorced ourselves, linking our future to forms of religious and technical thinking that placed us outside the nurture of cosmic rhythms.

Inside the submersible it is suddenly dark, as if the sun had been pinched from the sky. We are under the surface, in the rolling shadow of the mother ship. A blue light streams in through the three small viewports, throwing Anatoly's face into shadow.

Of all the acts that confirm our unconscious need to reconsider Nature, few are as symbolic as descending into the ocean. As scuba divers or inside roving submersibles, we step off the land, leaving behind our urban alliance with concrete and asphalt. Underwater, our survival hinges on containers of portable air. Inside this strange inner space, we become weightless, drifting toward our aquatic origins.

As trespassers in this other world, we are more susceptible to shifts in thinking and emotion. Our eyes are captured by unfamiliar colors and patterns of light and shadow. The pressurized air sliding in and out of our lungs reminds us of our mortality. And from this, it is not a large intuitive leap to consider the mortality of the planet.

The deep ocean is one of the last untouched places on Earth. With three miles (5 km) of water overhead, the twenty-first century seems like a rumor. Rich with scientific opportunities, the deep ocean is a place that suggests there are dimensions beyond reason. If we begin to think about what we are doing in the ocean—and the real implications of our actions—we will create a new philosophy, a philosophy of Nature.

The men and women whose writing and photographs grace this book have a philosophy that embraces Nature. They care about currents, waves and light. They care about animals and plants. They care about life.

They were drawn to the sea, I suspect, at an early age when, for them, the ocean was huge, inviting and so different from what they knew. They sensed adventure in it. From this initial contact came excitement, admiration and eventually the discipline and dedication that supports a career. But, in time, there also came a sense of loss. They saw the ocean changing. They saw depleted fish stocks and battered reefs. They heard about global warming, rising sea levels and radioactive wastes being dumped into the abyss.

And now they have joined their ideas and images together for a journey that will explore the marvel and mystery of the sea and the forces that cloud its future. They will warn us: only Earth, the third planet out from the sun, has oceans, from whose nourishing waters came the life that would become human. Only Earth has beings capable of destroying the watery realm that is the very guarantor of their survival.

We are now 330 feet (100 m) under the Atlantic. The Azores are over the horizon to the south. Directly below us is a slice in the crust of the Earth deeper than the Grand Canyon. From its bottom, under 16,000 feet (5,000 m) of water, we will climb the northern wall gathering rock samples that will help us understand the history and future of this part of the Atlantic. Outside, the ocean is becoming colder and darker. Inside, looking around at the submersible's blinking lights and panel switches, I feel as vulnerable as an astronaut inside his mechanical planet.

It is Anatoly, my Russian pilot, who gives me confidence. A former Cold War enemy, he is a symbol of the change that is reshaping our lives. Our earlier dives together have taught us that the future can be navigated successfully only by those who are willing to share.

What I sense in Anatoly and the people who created this book is a spiritual relationship with the ocean. On these pages they are translators of this experience for the rest of us.

Their message is that we need a soul-deep understanding of the place and history of the sea in human affairs. Knowing the ocean's relationship to art and literature, to the evolution of human personality, is vital. And, learning to love the sea for its own sake — without trying to measure its economic utility — is equally vital.

Once collected extensively for aquariums, the garibaldi (Hypsypops rubicundus) is now protected in California, USA, where it is the state marine fish.

ARCTIC OCEAN

Laptev Sea

East Siberian Sea

Chukchi Sea

Beaufort Sea

Victoria Island

Ellesmere Island

Greenland

Baffin Bay

Baffin Island

ARCTIC CIRCLE

ASIA

Sea of Okhotsk

Bering Sea

Gulf of Alaska

Queen Charlotte Islands

Hudson Bay

Labrador Sea

3

NORTH
AMERICA

St. Lawrence River

5

Vancouver Island

Newfoundland

Sea of Japan

Japan

4

6

Yellow Sea

PACIFIC OCEAN

East China Sea

1

TROPIC OF CANCER

Gulf of Mexico

Bahama Islands

Philippine Sea

Hawaiian Islands

Gulf of California

Cuba

Puerto Rico

Bay of Bengal

South
China
Sea

Philippine Islands

Hispaniola

Caribbean Sea

Sri Lanka

Borneo

Celebes Sea

EQUATOR

A

Sumatra

Java Sea

New Guinea

Micronesia

Galapagos Islands

SOUTH
AMERICA

Celebes

Java

Timor

Arafura Sea

Coral Sea

Polynesia

INDIAN

Timor Sea

2

TROPIC OF CAPRICORN

OCEAN

AUSTRALIA

Tasman Sea

N

Tasmania

New Zealand

ANTARCTIC CIRCLE

ANTARCTICA

Ross Sea

Amundsen Sea

Bellingshausen Sea

Weddell Sea

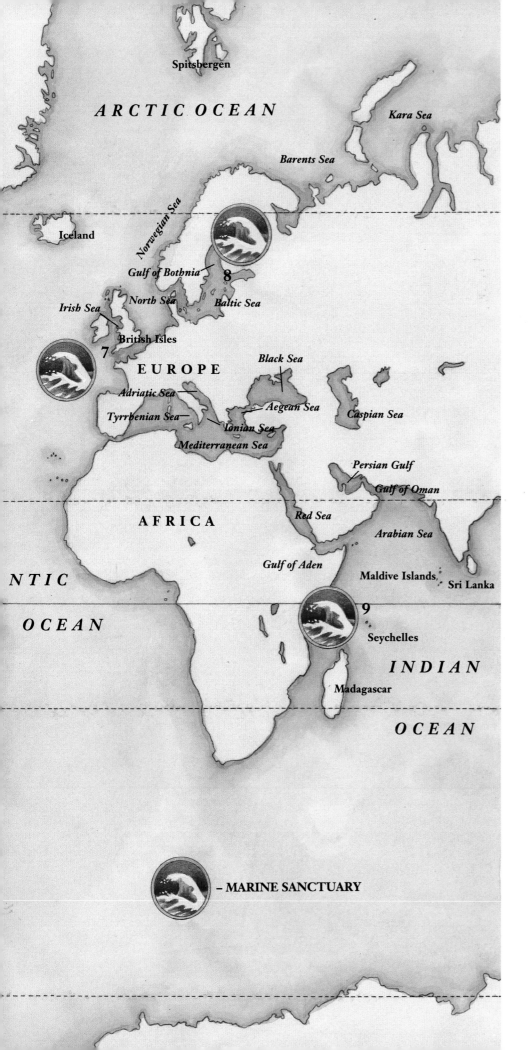

THE WORLD OCEAN

There are many hundreds of marine sanctuaries throughout the world ocean. Most have a land component; none are isolated from threats that originate outside the reserve on land or in the ocean or atmosphere. They can be categorized by the type of resource they are intended to protect, their size, how they are managed and the activities that are permitted within the sanctuary. Most are designed to protect coastal areas, islands or resources connected to the seafloor rather than open ocean areas. Some permit scientific and educational activities and commercial activities such as fishing and tourism. The following examples are representative of the types of marine sanctuaries found around the world.

1 Kuroshima Marine Park, Kuroshima Island, Japan

Japan's twenty-three small marine parks were selected for the beauty of their undersea scapes and protected in 1970 under revisions made to the National Parks Law. Kuroshima Marine Park has accommodation facilities, a marine research laboratory and a visitor interpretation centre. Japan's marine parks are heavily used for recreation and education.

2 The Great Barrier Reef Marine Park, Queensland, Australia

This park stretches along the northeast coast of Australia in a complex maze of approximately 2,500 individual coral reefs. It is protected under a specific act of the Australian government and is managed by an independent government authority. The park is zoned; some zones are designated for complete protection, others for commercial development, fishing, recreation or education.

3 South Moresby/Gwaii Haanas, British Columbia, Canada

This national marine park covers an area of over 1,850 square miles (4,800 km²). Canada's national marine parks policy provides for multiple use of reserve areas, including zones for habitat protection and zones for uses such as fishing, recreation and education.

4 Point Reyes-Farallon Islands National Marine Sanctuary, San Francisco, California, USA

This sanctuary, which covers 948 square nautical miles (3,250 km²), protects a variety of habitats, including salt marshes, shores and beaches, as well as ocean areas. It is protected under a number of state and federal laws and the National Marine Sanctuary Program.

5 Funk Island, Newfoundland, Canada

Funk Island is a breeding island for thousands of seabirds. It is protected under provincial government legislation. Access to the island is forbidden, except for rare scientific visits to monitor the birds' breeding activity. Protective jurisdiction does not apply to the surrounding ocean.

6 USS Monitor National Marine Sanctuary, Cape Hatteras, North Carolina, USA

This small sanctuary, located sixteen nautical miles (30 km) offshore, was established in 1975 under the National Marine Sanctuary Program, to protect the historic Civil War vessel, the USS Monitor. The site is administered by state and national agencies and a university.

7 Skomer Marine Reserve, Wales, United Kingdom

A nongovernmental trust was formed to protect this important seabird breeding island and the surrounding waters. The trust's volunteers produce educational materials, management plans and reports.

8 Jussaro Strict Nature Reserve and Tvarminne Zoological Station, Gulf of Bothnia, Finland

Access to the approximately eighty islands in this reserve is strictly controlled. However, the ocean area around the islands can be used by recreational boaters and fishermen. The University of Helsinki has a nearby zoological station, which protects a small ocean area for research.

9 Ste. Anne Marine National Park, Ste. Anne Island, Seychelles

A national conservation policy, adopted in 1971, is the basis for protection of marine areas in the Seychelles. Marine parks are designed to protect the coastal and marine habitats, while providing for traditional uses and tourism developments. In Ste. Anne Marine National Park, only long-time residents can fish within the park, and they must adhere to strict catch limits.

THE MEETING PLACE

HILLARY HAUSER

IN THE LATE NINETEEN SIXTIES, THE AMERICAN POET ROD McKUEN MADE a record album called "The Sea." Against a backdrop of waves and a single oboe, he speaks about friendship with the ocean: "If we want someone to know/We should get to know the sea."

These words have stayed with me because I swim in the ocean every day, even in stormy weather or the dead of winter. My favorite thing to do is to jump out of bed early in the morning and dive in with my pajamas on. I like the feel of the water, which is sometimes freezing cold. I like swimming across tangly kelp and smelling the plankton that sometimes gets in my hair. I like the solitude just beyond the breakers, where I can float on my back and look up at the nearby mountains. I like to ride a wave and get sand in my suit. When sea lions or dolphins swim by, I try to swim out and strike up a conversation.

Throughout time, many people have derived comfort from the sea in simple ways — walking along a seashore, contemplating the surf, watching seagulls dip and soar, getting their toes wet, playing with their dogs in the sand.

There is inspiration here, too. Artists have covered miles of canvas with crashing waves and sparkling inlets, and writers have produced volumes on the mysteries of the deep and the magic of the shore.

Whatever our profession or background, we all scramble to the beach for recreation and regeneration. We swim in the waves, fish in the surf, scuba dive along offshore reefs, and sail in boats around harbors and bays. We ask

Opposite:
Eel grass (Zostera marina) *helps to stabilize muddy shorelines and provides food and shelter for coastal animals.*

17

Sea horses (Hippocampus) are often found in tidepools, clinging to seaweed. Their inshore habitat makes these small fish vulnerable to local pollution, trawling and dredging.

JEFF FOOTT

for oceanfront hotel rooms, and in restaurants we request tables with a view of the water. In many countries, prospective house buyers pay a premium for every square inch of ocean view—even if that view is from a small window in a broom closet. There is no doubt about it—the seashore is precious.

The problem is, we may be loving our shorelines to death.

After I graduated from college I went to work for a magazine that had a publishing office in Los Angeles. I leased a small garage apartment on a local beach, where I swam in the sea every morning. I felt very fortunate to be able to do this. When I landed a month-long assignment in Mexico, I subleased my little place to a co-worker. On my return, I was amazed to learn that my friend had moved out after only a few days, "because it was too damp and the ocean was just too noisy!" I remember thinking at the time that maybe it was a good thing that some people did not like the beach. This left more of it for the rest of us who did.

Wishful thinking! The fact remains that a great many people want to be near the ocean. The result is an immense push on the shoreline. This drive to be near the sea has even been analyzed by some psychologists as an attempt to return to our origins. Conjecture aside, the world's population has swelled by about 1.2 billion people in the last fifteen years. If all of the coastline in the world, including the Arctic and Antarctic, is combined and divided by the Earth's population, approximately five inches (13 cm) of coastline exist for each person.

This depressing statement was made by the eminent American marine scientist Carleton Ray, who went on to say that five inches is "not much—in fact, you couldn't stand side by side, because most people are wider than five inches." He also noted that this swelling population has tended to congregate around important biological areas of the sea:

> Consider the fact that man has always gone to protected coves and harbors for development . . . nice protected places which are—or were—among the richest places for living resources in the world. So, the richest places in the world are also the most populated. . . . This leads to the extremely alarming fact that man, while he's increasing his numbers, is also decreasing the earth's coastal zone capacity to provide biological living materials for him, since estuarine places are nursery grounds for most forms of ocean life.

THE MAGIC OF ESTUARIES

Estuaries or wetlands — places where freshwater rivers and runoffs meet the sea — often appear as shallow swamps, rimmed with high marsh grasses and splotched with patches of algae growing on still waters. When the waters recede. they can look like soggy, pock-marked river bottoms. In some places, such as the Florida Everglades, the dominant vegetation is mangroves — tangled greenery that is flooded by a brackish mixture of fresh and salt water.

To the uninformed eye, estuaries may look stagnant, even unattractive. There was a time not long past, in fact, when people looked at such places and wanted to convert them into something more useful and attractive. Because estuaries are places where the sea encroaches inland, many of them have become prime sites for harbors. They have been dredged, which automatically fills them with salt water, and breakwaters have been built, with marinas for boats situated inside. Ship chandleries, fish markets and cafés have been erected to attract visitors. The largest estuaries of many countries are

This mangrove (Rhizophora) swamp is protected in Everglades National Park, Florida, USA. In some areas of the world, such as Bangladesh, so much mangrove forest has been destroyed on outer islands that storm surges caused by cyclones now move much further inland, resulting in destruction and loss of life.

Purple shore crabs (Hemigrapsus nudus) live in estuaries. The 4,500 species of true crabs range worldwide from shorelines to the abyss.

now important seaports, and those not replaced by a harbor or marina have been altered with some other type of waterfront development — condominiums, waterfront homes with boat docks, or oceanfront business areas, complete with hotels and restaurants offering rooms and tables with ocean views.

Marine science has only recently caught up with such developments. Research has shown that estuaries are important nursery grounds for two-thirds of all the animals that live in the sea. Young larval fish migrate to estuaries, where they find an abundance of food in the brackish water. These fish include colorful reef fish, as well as food and game fish such as snapper and tarpon. In the estuary, the young fish can grow in a safe environment free of ocean predators, until they are large enough to defend themselves in the open sea. Other estuary inhabitants that set up permanent homes in the muddy bottom include clams, oysters, mussels, and some types of shrimp.

By stripping our coastlines of estuaries, we have inadvertently stripped ourselves of entire unknown populations of marine animals and a potential food supply. However, despite this scientific revelation, estuaries and wetlands are still being destroyed in the name of "progress." As this book goes to press, the Sheraton Hotel in Nadi, Fiji, is bulldozing acres of mangroves to build golf courses. In the United States, the Walt Disney Company proposes to fill in 250 acres (100 ha) of land along California's Long Beach shoreline for the building of a $3-billion amusement park.

Three-quarters of American wetlands are owned by coastal developers, individual farmers and large landholders. Although such areas are major nesting and roosting areas for many species of ducks, habitats for small animals, and vital nursery and breeding grounds for many types of fish, an estimated 290,000 acres (117,000 ha) of wetlands are being lost each year. In August 1991, U.S. president George Bush held out a life preserver, a policy paper authorizing the purchase of as much as 1 million acres (400,000 ha) of wetlands. The policy paper also proposed to expand research and to restore some wetlands on federal property.

Unfortunately, the policy paper had some holes in it. It revised the definition of "wetland," which critics said would expose millions of acres to development. It also included a proposal to speed up the approval process for development. Bush defended his policy as balancing two factors: it would protect the wetlands, while allowing for sustained economic growth and development. To some, this mixing of philosophies is untenable. Economics always seems to win in the end.

Similarly, when the French ocean explorer and filmmaker Jean-Michel Cousteau told a large tourism convention in Fiji that the destruction of mangroves to make golf courses would rob the world of fish, there was a major stir among the locals against his statement. "Fish? — the Fijians have enough fish!" said one. "There are miles and miles of mangroves here. The Fijians need jobs. This development is giving the Fijians jobs!" Not surprisingly, Third World countries have a difficult time understanding how rich nations, which have produced wealth by exploiting their own environments, can ask them to stay poor and preserve theirs. Can the Fijians be convinced that tourists might be persuaded to visit a wildlife preserve rather than play golf? Only time will tell.

The estuaries of the world are not only threatened by direct digging, dredging or filling. Their waters are also changing in character, with the result that many forms of estuary life cannot survive in them. Freshwater rivers flowing to the sea are being dammed at alarming rates, to harness water for power, agriculture, irrigation and drinking. It has been estimated that by the year 2000 about two-thirds of the world's total flow of water to the ocean

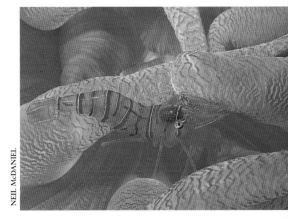

Estuaries, which are being drained or altered in many parts of the world, are an important nursery for many species of shrimp, including this candy-stripe shrimp (Lebbeus grandimanus)*, which lives in the northern Pacific.*

The crown of thorns starfish
(Acanthaster planc*i) preys on
living coral. Population explosions, possibly due to human
removal of their predators, have
destroyed parts of Australia's
Great Barrier Reef and other
coral reefs in the Pacific.*

will be controlled by dams. When freshwater is withheld from the sea, the saline content of estuary waters soars. The shrimp, oysters, mussels and fish that live in coastal wetlands cannot survive in high-salinity water.

What scientists are now realizing, with their more sophisticated instruments and increased knowledge, is that seawater is a finely tuned combination of elements. They have also come to know that everything in the sea is connected. When one thing is changed in the ocean, a ripple effect occurs—something else happens down the line.

Such an effect can be seen in the spreading eutrophication of the world's shorelines. Rivers are emptying vast quantities of pollutants into the sea, the result of storm runoffs from cities and countrysides. Excessive nutrients, such as phosphates, find their way to the ocean this way, and cause algae blooms where they settle. Algae consume oxygen from the water. When vast quantities are present, the resident fish fail to get their fair share of oxygen and they die.

Massive fish kills along the beaches of countries around the world are now commonplace. The sardine fishery of the eastern Mediterranean perished because of algae bloom. In the Albemarle and Pamlico sounds of North Carolina, low levels of dissolved oxygen in water have suffocated hundreds of thousands of striped bass, crabs and eels. Puget Sound in Washington State is battling similar problems. Dead fish, algae and nursery grounds turned into graves—it is a sad story told along too many of our shorelines.

THE WORLD OF THE REEF

Around every continent and island in the world is a submerged "shelf" that angles up to the shore. Some shelves are wide, some narrow. Some drop off precipitously into a deep abyss and some stretch out so gradually that ten miles (16 km) out from the beach you might find yourself in only one hundred feet (30 m) of water.

Of all the zones of the sea, the continental shelf is the most fertile because it receives more sunlight than the other zones. In the ocean, as on land, the

sun's energy is used by plants in the process of photosynthesis. Through this chemical process, marine plants grow and become food for many fish and other marine life forms. In the tropics, the sun encourages the growth of coral.

Not long ago, I was decompressing from a deep scuba dive on the Great White Wall at Taveuni, Fiji. On a shallow, fringing coral reef I waited at ten feet (3 m), and with time to spend, I began watching everything around me in detail. I studied the colorful fish darting in and out of knotty coral branches, and teased the little wrasses that alternately picked at my fingers and peeked into my faceplate.

In the distance I could see the waves breaking on the reef. As I watched the white bubble-and-foam action of the surf from this underwater viewpoint, I could not help but reflect on how these semisubmerged coral reefs do such a fine job of protecting nearby islands from the fury of ocean storms. The enormous fields of spun coral diffuse and break up the force of waves that roll across the open sea.

At over 1,000 miles (1,600 km) in length, the Great Barrier Reef off the northeast coast of Australia is the largest coral reef system in the world. The Great Barrier Reef Marine Park Authority oversees its conservation.

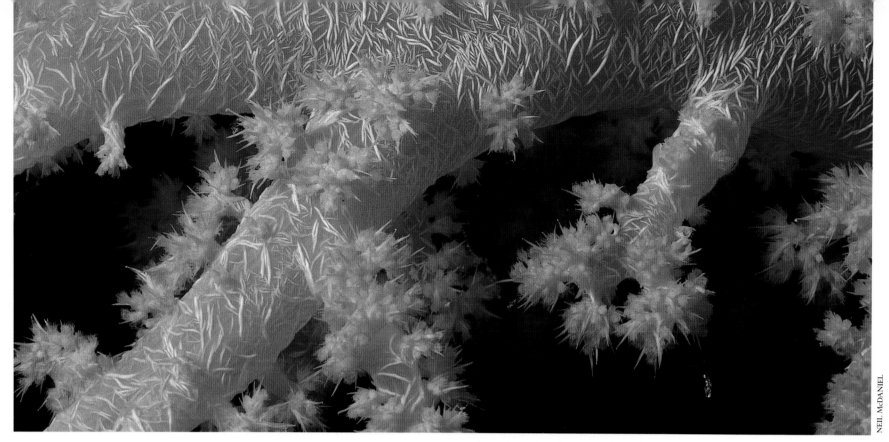

A closeup of the polyps of soft coral (Dendronephthya *sp.*). *Unlike stony corals, the fragile soft-bodied corals do not build reefs.*

Coral reefs are among the most beautiful and diverse gardens of life on our planet. Like those "magic rocks" that many of us played with as children, coral seems to have magically fizzed and solidified into miniature castles upon contact with water. These castles do not appear to be animal in origin, but they are. Coral reefs are composed of the delicate, calcified structures of tiny anemone-like creatures, which slowly but surely build upon each other, generation after generation.

There are two important factors in this living and building process: sunlight and clean water. The coral polyps extend their tentacles into the passing currents to strain out plankton, which they feed upon. They rely on the sun and the process of photosynthesis to encourage the growth of the symbiotic dinoflagellates and algae that provide them with oxygen and with the lime they use for their skeletons. Dredging, which often occurs during the construction of tropical hotels and marinas, spreads silt over a coral reef, smothering the tiny animals.

The importance of coral reefs cannot be overstated: they not only provide the lands they surround with protection from open-ocean storms, but underwater they provide protective homes for millions upon millions of fish and invertebrates. Large pelagic fish, such as the tuna and jack, swim into the shallow reef communities to feed on the resident sea life, a fact well known by fishermen around the world. Among the most important biological sites of the planet, reefs serve both as protection and pantry.

They are also a joy. Scuba divers everywhere have discovered, by the hundreds of thousands, the colorful magic of these coral kingdoms. Yet one diver stepping on a coral branch can break off in less than a second what coral animals have taken eons to create. With hordes of underwater visitors exploring a reef site day after day, year after year, these little breakages can add up to serious degradation. The anchoring of boats on the reef adds to the damage.

Dr. Ray, who proposed with Ilia A. Tolstoy the first land-and-sea park in the world, the Exuma Cays Land and Sea Park in the Bahamas (created through the Bahamas National Trust), explains the problem this way:

> It's what we call carrying capacity. Just as a field can hold just so many cows, so a reef can hold just so many divers without damage. It's not sufficient to protect a reef from spearfishing and the collecting of corals, seafans and shells. The very presence of continuous, high-intensity use disturbs fish and corals, [and] causes some breakage of delicate coral structures.

The solution, he says, is through management plans to give some reefs "diver relief" from time to time. Many terrestrial parks have had to do this to protect wildlife habitats, and there is no reason why similar management plans could not be developed for threatened ocean areas. Many of today's scuba divers are aware of their effects on the reef environment. They are learning to use buoyancy vests more so that they kick less, and they are adopting a hands-off policy when swimming around the corals they have come to see.

THE SOLUTION TO POLLUTION

There was a saying in the 1950s and 1960s that was supposed to be clever but that revealed an astonishing attitude toward the sea: "The solution to pollution is dilution." In other words, take all the waste you do not know what to do with and simply dump it into the sea. It was thought that the ocean was capable of diluting and absorbing vast amounts of liquid and solid waste.

Bay pipefish (Syngnathus lep-torhynchus), *Puget Sound, USA. These aptly named fish have bony plates encasing their bodies instead of scales. Because these fish generally inhabit inshore areas, they are vulnerable to coastal pollution.*

Following pages:
Starfish, which are also called sea stars, are echinoderms, members of a widespread group of animals that exists only in the sea. FREEMAN PATTERSON

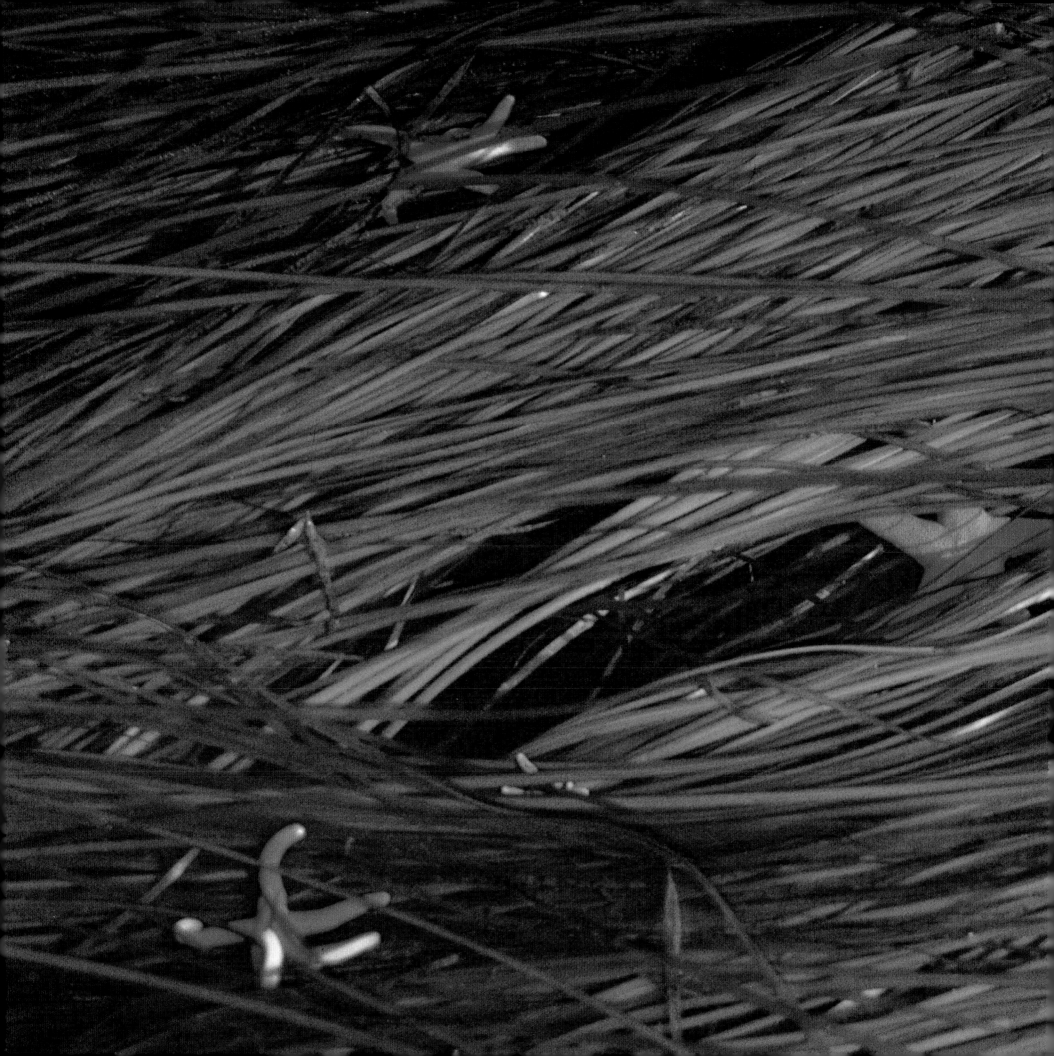

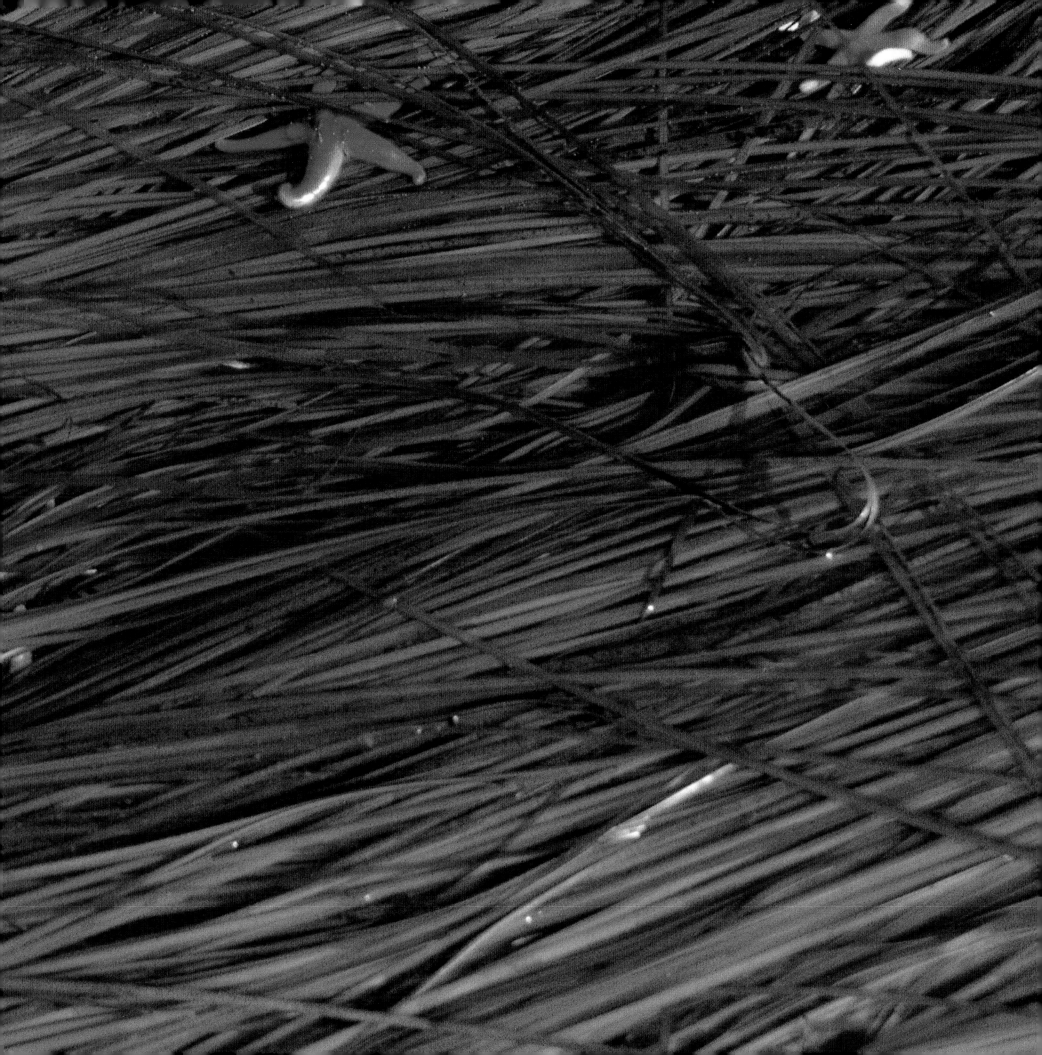

Hermit crabs can be seen in shallow coastal waters throughout the world. This species, Pagurus granosimanus, *occurs on the west coast of North America. To protect their soft bodies, hermit crabs find and wear an empty shell, which they exchange for a larger one several times during their lives as they grow.*

As idiotic as this practice sounds on paper, we are doing it daily. We are dumping into the sea everything from radioactive waste to sewage. The errors of this solution-is-dilution practice became painfully obvious in Minamata, Japan, in the 1950s and 1960s. Beginning in 1953, the people of this small coastal town began to suffer strange neurological diseases, which ended in death for many. It took years to trace the cause to fish and shellfish overloaded with a lethal form of mercury. Fingers were pointed at a manufacturing plant that discharged its wastes—including mercury—into Minamata Bay. However, the mercury sent into the sea by the plant was inorganic and relatively safe when ingested in small doses, while the deadly mercury that poisoned the people was organic. For the time being, the manufacturer was absolved of any responsibility. It was not until 1967 that scientists discovered that the sea is able to transform the properties of chemical substances from safe to toxic. The mercury of Minamata Bay, ingested by the fish and shellfish, had been transformed into deadly poison.

In the shallow waters of the shoreline, where rich fishing industries thrive, it seems inconceivable that we would dump lethal wastes. And, in fact, these wastes are usually deposited in deep water. But sometimes substances dumped into water far offshore end up in shallow water. Thirty miles (48 km) west of San Francisco, California, 47,500 steel barrels containing chemicals such as plutonium, cesium and mercury have been scattered over an undersea area of more than 350 square miles (900 km²). Scientists are now trying to determine whether these cannisters have broken open, and if their lethal contents have reached the Point Reyes-Farallon Islands National Marine Sanctuary, one of the richest marine habitats in the world.

The most insidious form of ocean dumping in shallow coastal waters is dredging. It has been estimated that 80 percent of all ocean dumping in the world is the result of dredging harbors, which tend to silt in and fill up, becoming too shallow for visiting ships. The toxic waste and bacteria that accumulate at the bottom of a harbor for months are suddenly dug up and spewed out in the ocean currents that travel down the coast. There is evidence that fish are contaminated by this practice, but some scientists argue that the toxic heavy metals accumulate in the guts of fish, while the edible parts remain free of contamination. This reasoning might be fine if one assumes all people are like fugu chefs, highly trained Japanese cooks who know how to avoid the parts of the fugu blowfish that can kill a person outright. Unfortunately, not many of us are.

Another problem for nearshore areas of the sea occurs on a daily basis in the form of sewage and sewage sludge. In the United States alone, an estimated 8 billion gallons (30 billion L) of municipal sewage are discharged each day into coastal waters. Too large a percentage of it is raw and untreated. Sewage sludge is a mix of solid human waste, viruses and pathogenic bacteria, along with carcinogenic chemicals such as PCBs and heavy metals. In addition to the effluent from sewage treatment plants, sludge contains waste from city streets that is washed into sewers. This includes oil and grease, along with heavy metals such as mercury, lead, copper and cadmium, which accumulate in marine organisms and poison the people who eat the contaminated seafood.

The most commonly accepted way to dispose of sewage has been to pipe treated sewage into the sea, very often in nearshore areas. Sewage effluent either gets primary, secondary or tertiary treatment. "Primary" treatment means the solids have been removed from the effluent; "secondary" means the effluent has been chlorinated to kill bacteria; and "tertiary" means that the effluent has gone through additional processing that renders it suitable for agricultural use.

The subject of sewage disposal in the ocean became of paramount interest to me during the six years I covered commercial fishing and other marine subjects for a Santa Barbara, California, newspaper. There are five sewage plants in the area that dump their effluents into the Santa Barbara Channel, an important commercial fishing ground.

One day in 1987 an alarming report came across my desk. The report stated that California's seafood might become inedible within three years because of sewage. Issued by the U.S. Office of Technology Assessment (an investigative arm of Congress), the report stated that harmful bacteria occurring in human waste do not die off quickly, as scientists had long believed. Instead, the bacteria lie dormant until they find a suitable medium in which to grow, such as the stomachs of fish and shellfish, where they return to their

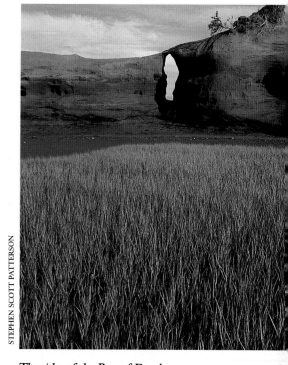

STEPHEN SCOTT PATTERSON

The tides of the Bay of Fundy in eastern Canada, which are the largest in the world, sculpt sandstone formations along the coast. This formation was photographed in July at low tide.

A wreck lies on a beach in Queensland, Australia. Countless wrecks have been abandoned on the shores and in the waters of the world ocean. Among them are seven nuclear submarines.

previous "fully virulent form." The report noted that more than 1 billion gallons (4 billion L) of sewage were being dumped each day off the California coast, and that commercial harvesting of seafood was already prohibited or partially restricted in about one-third of California's productive shellfish areas because of contamination.

I was angry. I decided to conduct a local "sewage roundup," to see what our area was contributing to this mess. I learned that Santa Barbara was dumping about 16 million gallons (61 million L) of sewage effluent into the Santa Barbara Channel each day. I asked the managers of the five sewage treatment plants exactly what it was they were dumping, and where. It was like pulling teeth to get this information from them, and no wonder. I learned that millions of gallons of secondarily treated sewage were being poured daily in less than one hundred feet (30 m) of water within one or two miles (1.5 or 3 km) of popular swimming beaches. Unbelievably, one outfall was in 35 feet (11 m) of water only 1,500 feet (460 m) off a beach in front of an elegant hotel.

I talked to marine biologists studying the kelp beds in the channel. They told me that although the once-prolific forests of giant brown kelp (*Macrocystis pyrifera*) had been severely damaged by the El Niño storms of 1983, they suspected the real reason for their decline was the continued dumping of sewage in nearshore waters.

Amid all this depressing news was a single shining light: there is one pilot treatment plant serving a community in the Los Angeles area that is giving its effluent tertiary treatment. Everything produced from the Fountain Valley plant is used for irrigation and agriculture.

Today, too many coastal communities around the world are closing beaches and advising swimmers to stay out of the water because it is polluted by sewage and storm water runoff. I think of this and of the Fountain Valley treatment plant that gives its effluent tertiary treatment, and I cannot help but think that many of us would not mind paying an additional monthly fee for such treatment—for the privilege of knowing that at least what goes down our household pipes is not adding to the ocean's ills. The solution to the pollution is simply to stop doing it.

THE PROBLEM OF OIL

This sign on a deserted beach in Gdansk, Poland, warns of pollution.

It used to be that oil companies drilled for oil primarily on land. There was a simple reason for this: the human hand was the best instrument to deal with the valves and flanges of oil platforms. With the development of under-water technology, however, oil operations moved offshore. In fact, the spread of oil fields at sea followed the depths to which man could dive. Now that there are Remote Operated Vehicles (ROVs) and one-man submersibles with high-tech manipulators for hands, oil platforms are being installed in deeper and deeper water — even on the Outer Continental Shelf. Whether shallow or deep, the coastlines of some countries are rimmed with giant steel platforms.

Seals (family Otariidae) congregate on a buoy in the Santa Barbara Channel, California, USA. An oil platform stands in the background. Some seal species are able to coexist with humans, taking advantage of man-made objects to haul out on or stealing fish from nets, while others, such as the monk seals (Monachus), are less able to tolerate human disturbance of their shoreline habitat.

The most visible environmental problem of offshore oil operations is the oil spill — tar-black or rainbow-greasy slicks coating the surface of the sea. Notable platform spills range from the 1969 blowout of Union Oil platform A off Santa Barbara, California, which poured 2 million gallons (7.5 million L) of oil into the Santa Barbara Channel, to the Ixtoc blowout in Campeche Bay, Mexico, which spilled 140 million gallons (530 million L). Oil tankers have come to grief on the shorelines of the world, too — from the *Amoco Cadiz* off Brittany in 1978 (68.7 million gallons of oil/260 million L) to the *Exxon Valdez* off Alaska in 1990 (11 million gallons/42 million L). It has been estimated that somewhere between 3 and 7 million tons of oil are spilled into the ocean each year. Much of it ends up on the beaches and the rest sinks to the bottom, poisoning the creatures that live there.

Processes for cleaning up an oil spill are woefully inadequate, and in some cases may present problems worse than the oil spill itself. For example, the chemical dispersants used to force the oil beneath the surface (an out-of-sight, out-of-mind approach to cleaning up) have proven to be more toxic to marine life than the oil itself. And after the *Exxon Valdez* catastrophe, it was learned that the high-pressure spraying of the shoreline actually stripped the coast of small plant and animal life.

Although oil spills are ugly and tragic, a more insidious and hidden form of oil pollution is the subsurface dumping of drilling muds from oil platforms. Drilling mud (more correctly called drilling fluid) is a clay-based (barite) fluid used to lubricate the drill bit, circulate the drill cuttings to the surface, help seal the well wall, and control pressure in the well. Lubricants and other substances are added to the "mud," including arsenic, cadmium, chromium and mercury, all highly toxic.

By itself, the oil platform does not harm the environment. The prolific plankton, drifting on the open seas, cruise into the platform area and settle on its steel legs. Very soon after the platform is installed, in fact, it begins to function as an artificial reef. The legs become covered with mussels, crabs, starfish, sea anemones and sponges. Then the fish arrive to feed on the resident creatures.

I have made many dives under the oil platforms in the Santa Barbara

Channel. For years, I recorded and wrote about the underwater life that congregates on the legs of these structures. My photographer friend Bob Evans and I documented a cabezon (*Scorpaenichthys marmoratus*), a California fish, laying its eggs on the cross-pilings of a platform, and we observed starfishes and crabs battling for space and food. One day, however, underneath a platform where we had spent hours recording an abundance of marine life, Bob discovered a devastating seascape of decay and death. The bottom was covered with drill mud. He reported his discovery to the oil company that owned the platform, but his reports were ignored. They were also ignored by the governmental agencies overseeing the oil company's operations.

Not long after Bob discovered the accidental dumping of drill mud under the platform we knew so well, oil companies operating in the area applied for blanket permits to dump drill mud in the Santa Barbara Channel. They already had permits to dump this waste in federal waters, which are three miles (5 km) out, but in state waters closer to shore, it had to be hauled to a toxic waste dump on land. The oil companies wanted to bypass the expensive and time-consuming process of barging the drill mud to shore.

I again went to work on an investigative piece for my newspaper. I attended numerous hearings, where I listened to biologists (hired by the oil companies) state that sea life can withstand the dumping of drill mud at sea. They acknowledged poisoning and immediate smothering of animals near the platforms, but said such damage is "temporary, and the marine animals quickly recolonize." I read voluminous environmental studies that said most of the drill mud drifts down-current, dispersing the offensive elements in such a way that they are not hazardous. The fact that these poisons can be ingested by marine life and transformed into toxics lethal to humans (as in the Minamata disaster) was not addressed in these studies, and neither was the effect of drill mud on plankton.

Since plankton are not easily seen with the human eye, they can be easily overlooked by those who choose to overlook them. However, since they are also the building blocks for all marine animals, entire populations can be killed off when the life processes of the invisible plankton are interrupted. During the drill mud issue, Daniel E. Morse, a professor of molecular genetics

FREEMAN PATTERSON

Coastlines are in a constant state of change brought about by erosion, deposition and sea level changes. This erosion formation is found near Port Campbell, Victoria, Australia.

and biochemistry as well as a marine researcher, came to the plankton's defense. He pointed out that their finely tuned system of chemical transmitters and receptors was completely blocked by the dumping of drill mud. He summed up the issue this way:

> Typically, adult animals and plants exposed [to drill muds] for a short amount of time will probably live. But more important is the very critical life-cycle stage of marine animals that depend on settling of the very young larvae to grow into adults. . . . What they [oil companies] don't tell you is that the sea life that survives where drilling muds have been dumped are worms and things of that nature. Hundreds of different worms could be described as a "rich biological community," but is that what society wants?

The black-necked stilt (Himan-topus himantopus) inhabits the shorelines of all continents. Shorebirds are particularly sus-ceptible to coastal pollution.

JEFF FOOTT

ROLL ON, THOU DEEP AND DARK BLUE OCEAN

In 1955, when my family moved to the seashore in Santa Barbara, it was quite a different shore than it is now. As children, my brother, sister and I liked to play in front of the hotel down the beach. We would congregate with our friends at the lifeguard station at the foot of the stairs to the sand. On one side of the stairs was a children's playground with a big slide and swings. On the other side was a raked beach where adults sat in neat rows of backrests.

As I walk this same beach today, I find it hard to believe it is the one I knew as a child. The large stairway was replaced long ago by a small set of steps descending sideways from the boardwalk rather than straight toward the sea. The slide and swings for the children and the lifeguard station have also been relegated to memory.

The reason for this change is simple. The sea regularly storms under the boardwalk, sometimes once or twice a day. In 1955, this occurred during an occasional winter storm, but rarely in the summer. Today sea levels are higher, beaches are narrower, and beach houses and other waterfront developments are often "hammered" by the ocean.

One reason given for skinnier beaches is the damming of rivers. Less and less sand is being deposited at river mouths for transportation downcoast.

STEPHEN SCOTT PATTERSON

Canada has the longest ocean coastline in the world. This particular beach on the Atlantic side of Cape Breton Island, Nova Scotia, is protected in a national park called Cape Breton Highlands National Park.

Another theory concerns the higher concentration of carbon dioxide in the Earth's atmosphere, or the greenhouse effect. Because carbon dioxide traps heat, this increase is warming up the planet. With this rise in temperature, the ocean is also rising. Glaciers will begin to melt and retreat, adding to a further elevation of the world's sea levels. Inevitably, the warming water will occupy more space, which will contribute to the ocean's unstoppable march inland. The U.S. Environmental Protection Agency (EPA) estimates that with present warming trends, the world's sea levels will have risen from four to seven feet (1 to 2 m) by the year 2100.

A sea-level rise of this magnitude could mean that the Maldive Islands in the Indian Ocean, now about six feet (1.8 m) above sea level, would disappear.

Opposite and above:
On the Maldive Islands in the Indian Ocean, the removal of coral rock from the surrounding reefs to use as building material and fill has meant a loss of habitat for species dependent on coral. The elimination of part of the protective reef has also caused increased erosion of the small islands.

Starfish are frequently encountered in the intertidal zone. Some, like the Evasterias troscheli *shown here, are known for the considerable force they can exert with their suction-cupped tube feet to pull apart the shells of clams and other bivalves.*

Storms would drive an angry ocean inland to regularly flood Bangladesh and the Nile delta in Egypt. A sea-level rise of four feet (1 m) would submerge marshes, sounds and bays, push into river mouths, shove coastlines inland, and penetrate underground coastal aquifers everywhere.

If such a scenario comes to pass — and many scientists are saying it will — there is little we can do about it. Already there are discussions about constructing barrier islands, or dikes and levees such as already exist in Holland. However, Bill McKibben, in his excellent book, *The End of Nature*, points out that such measures may be self-defeating. Existing estuaries would be flushed by the new, advancing sea levels. If we construct walls, dikes and levees to protect oceanfront properties, these would prohibit the formation of new marshes or wetlands. Instead of the ocean "meeting the land with ease and grace," McKibben writes, it will bump into "an endless cement wall."

There are critics who scoff at the idea of irreversible warming and sea-level rise, who say that the ocean has always "run in cycles." Scientists admit that accurate measurements might not be possible until the year 2000, but by then the rise in both temperature and sea levels may be irreversible. Many scientists, though, are taking the carbon dioxide problem seriously, and are meeting in workshops to consider various solutions. They talk about fertilizing the oceans around Antarctica, to increase microscopic plant life there that uses carbon dioxide drawn from the air. They talk about growing millions of square miles of seaweeds that consume carbon dioxide. And they talk about collecting billions of pounds of carbon dioxide from the world's power plants and pumping it into the deepest oceans, where they think the gas might solidify and stay put.

Some people find a strange sense of comfort in the idea that the sea could someday reclaim much of the land we thought was ours. It is disconcerting and enlightening at the same time to think that the ocean might, in the end, defy human technology. Many people meditating at the shorelines where the land meets the sea come to the same realization: there is nothing that can withstand the power of a mighty ocean wave. It is this same power that stirred Lord Byron to write:

Roll on, thou deep and dark blue Ocean—roll!
Ten thousand fleets sweep over thee in vain;
Man marks the earth with ruin, his control
Stops with the shore; upon the watery plain
The wrecks are all thy deed, nor doth remain
A shadow of man's ravage, save his own,
When for a moment, like a drop of rain,
He sinks into thy depths with bubbling groan,
Without a grave, unknelled, uncoffined and unknown.

Wave action forms rock arches, such as this one in Cabo San Lucas, Mexico, by deepening caves on either side of a headland until they join.

Perspectives are needed at this hour. There are energy sources other than oil—including harnessing the tidal power of the sea—but these technologies require serious development. In the meantime, the industries operating upon or near the sea must be honest about what they are doing to it. There should be a willingness to pay whatever it takes to stop industrial poisoning of nearshore waters. The technology exists for reclaiming our sewage and wastes, but this reclamation costs money. Yet should we not be willing to spend this money, knowing that the ocean is capable of feeding the world? I am reminded of Rod McKuen telling us that the sea is our friend. The sea has given us so much. Can we not treat a friend more kindly?

ORIGINS
MARIE THARP

I N THE NINETEEN FIFTIES, RACHEL CARSON WROTE IN HER WONDERFUL book, *The Sea Around Us*, "Beginnings are apt to be shadowy, and so it is with the beginnings of that great mother of life, the sea." Today, the origins of the oceans are still a mystery. Standing beside those ancient waters, we can only imagine what took place millions of years ago. Theories abound. It used to be thought that the Earth had been formed from a whirling mass of gases, which had been sucked away from the sun, perhaps by a passing star. The gases cooled, liquefied and then hardened, and as the new crust cooled, vapor in the atmosphere condensed and rain began to fall, filling the ocean basins. Other scientists suggested that huge clouds of gas and dust particles had joined together and contracted to make the planet. The heat produced in this process gradually abated, and as the Earth cooled, the deluge began. Yet another theory speculates that water was collected within the planet as it formed and was released by volcanic activity.

We do know that after its birth, our planet did not consist of the seven continents we all learned about in school. Two hundred million years ago, all of the continents were united, forming one great land mass known as Pangaea. Surrounding this supercontinent was Panthalassa, the primordial ocean. During the Jurassic Period about 195 to 135 million years ago, Pangaea began to separate and drift apart, and Panthalassa's waters were divided into separate oceanic areas.

The existence of Pangaea was speculated about hundreds of years ago, but only recently accepted by the scientific community. In the early 1600s,

Opposite:
Lava flowing into the sea from Kilauea Volcano, Hawaii, USA.

UNDERWATER FEATURES

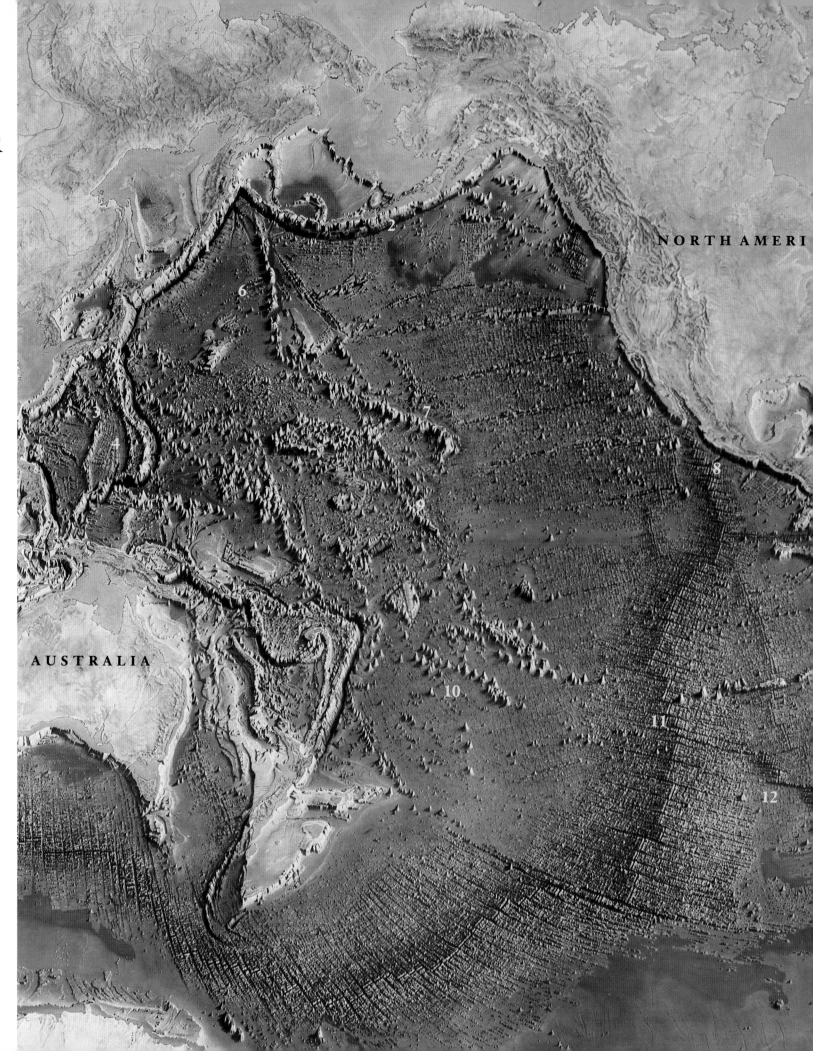

NORTH AMERI

AUSTRALIA

WORLD OCEAN FLOOR

By Bruce C. Heezen and Marie Tharp
Lamont Doherty Geological Observatory,
Palisades, N.Y. 10964
*Based on research and exploration initiated and supported by the
United States Navy Office of Naval Research*

Mercator Projection
Horizontal scale 1:23,230,300

1977

*Published by the United States Navy as a memorial to
Dr. Bruce C. Heezen in recognition of his contribution to man's
knowledge of the world ocean floor.*

EUROPE

ASIA

AFRICA

SOUTH AMERICA

ANTARCTICA

14

15

16

17

18

19

20

21

22

23

Sir Francis Bacon, the English philosopher, noticed that South America and Africa, when placed side by side, seemed to interlock as two pieces of a giant geographic puzzle, but he was unable to explain this phenomenon. In 1858, the French Biblical scholar and scientist Antonio Snider-Pelligrini wrote about the "split continents," which he believed were caused by Noah's Flood. Even Charles Darwin, who is better known for his work in biology than geology, noticed the split. He attributed it to a period of rapid rotation of the Earth, which had resulted in a portion of the planet being torn off and thrown into space to become the moon. He speculated that, during this event, the remaining crust of the Earth had been pulled apart.

In 1910, Alfred Wegener, a German meteorologist and geophysicist, developed the theory of the one-time existence of a supercontinent and called it Pangaea after Gaea, the mythological Greek "earth mother." This inevitably led him to his theory of continental drift. Following World War I, he began testing his hypothesis. First, he collected soil, fossil and rock samples from the coasts of Africa and South America. He was not surprised to find similar minerals in the soils and a correlation in the fossil samples found in both Brazil and Africa. Then he went on to show the similarities in the mountains of South America and those of Africa. And, finally, he theorized that a glacier similar to the one covering Antarctica today once covered the lower portion of Pangaea. Rock samples from lower South America and the southern part of Africa included soils, minerals and fossils not unlike those found in India, Australia and Antarctica. Soon after, he discovered yet another piece of the puzzle when he found that a plateau in Brazil fit together perfectly with one on Africa's Ivory Coast.

On January 6, 1912, Wegener presented his findings to the Geological Survey in Marburg, Germany, in a paper entitled "Die Entstehung der Kontinente und Ozeane" (The origins of continents and oceans). His theory was not given the reception he anticipated. Although it was viewed with interest in Europe, it was met with skepticism and antagonism in North America. The American scientists argued over such trivia as the ill fit of Newfoundland in Wegener's configuration and the lack of a "convincing force" to propel

*Representing a lineage once thought to be extinct, a coelacanth (*Latimeria chalumnae*) was first caught and identified by scientists in 1938. Fossil coelacanths date from the Devonian Period, 400 to 360 million years ago, and are thought to be precursors of land vertebrates.*

the continents. In the years to follow, no scientist would dare mention Wegener's theory since uttering such blasphemy could put one's career in jeopardy.

THE MID-ATLANTIC RIDGE

About fifty years before Wegener developed his theory, the first map showing the submarine topography of the North Atlantic was produced. In 1854, Matthew Fontaine Maury, the first director of the U.S. Navy Depot of Charts and Instruments, produced a map of the North Atlantic based upon about two hundred rope-and-lead-weight soundings. (This method of taking soundings, when compared with today's sophisticated techniques, was very primitive. A two-hundred-pound [90-kg] weight attached to a rope was lowered by a manually operated winch. The effort required to take a single sounding was so great that soundings were taken only every one hundred miles

Following pages:
*Lettuce coral (*Pachyseris *sp.), Truk Lagoon, Micronesia. Corals are ancient inhabitants of the ocean; they first developed in the Ordovician Period, 500 to 445 million years ago.*
NEIL McDANIEL

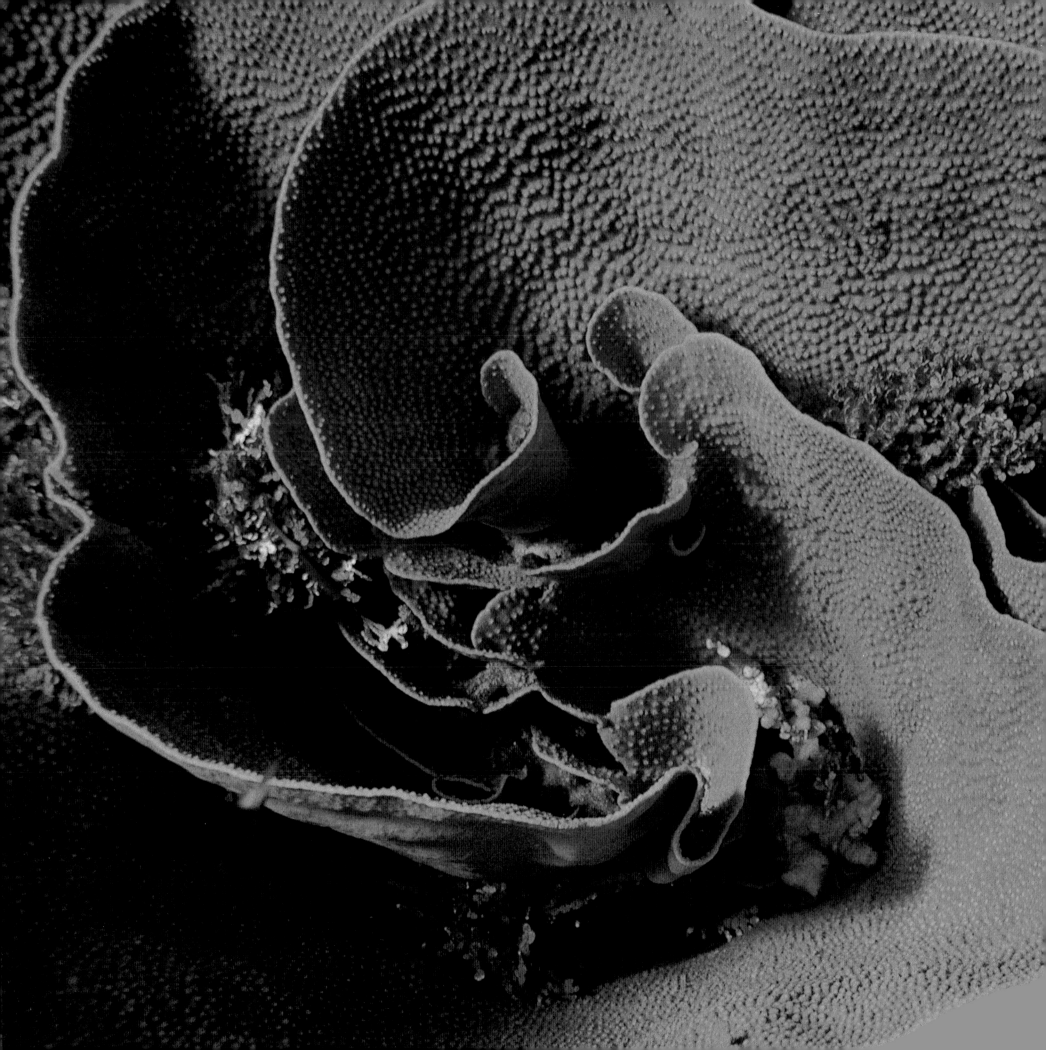

[160 km].) The contours appearing on Maury's map revealed a broad rise in the middle of the North Atlantic. He called this feature the Dolphin Rise. It was the first evidence that the mid-Atlantic seafloor was not a huge, featureless saucer filled with mud, as had been previously thought.

In 1872, the British ship HMS *Challenger* began a three-and-a-half-year expedition around the world taking soundings and water and biological samples. Widely spaced soundings confirmed a broad ridge in the middle of the North Atlantic, as did differences in the temperature of water on either side of it. The head scientist on board, Charles Wyville Thomson, concluded from soundings taken farther south than Maury's readings that the ridge was a continuous feature extending down to the equator.

From 1925 to 1927, the German ship *Meteor* surveyed the Atlantic Ocean. The primary purpose of this voyage was to chart the ocean currents and measure the properties of seawater, such as temperature, salinity and density. The researchers also took soundings five to twenty-five miles (8 to 40 km) apart using the "stopwatch-bang" method. This was an early use of echo soundings to determine the depth of the ocean. Numerous east-west crossings produced profiles of the bottom topography, which confirmed the existence of the Mid-Atlantic Ridge. Temperature readings also corroborated the differences in water temperature between the east and west basins of the Atlantic previously reported by the *Challenger* researchers. The *Meteor* expedition, however, determined that the ridge extended from the equator far down into the South Atlantic.

Alfred Wegener eagerly awaited the publication of the *Meteor* expedition's findings. Unfortunately, in 1929, he fell into a glacier crevasse while doing research in Greenland and died. The *Meteor* voyage received widespread publicity in the press in Europe and America, but the published scientific data lay neglected in various libraries until after World War II.

After the war ended, a number of geologists and geophysicists began researching the ocean floor. Bruce C. Heezen was a graduate student in geology at Columbia University in New York working closely with Maurice Ewing. Their first breakthrough was the discovery that the ocean floor could be divided into smooth and rough areas. As a result of their first expedition

on the *Atlantis I* research vessel in the late 1940s, it was recognized that this difference in the smooth relief and the rough relief of the seafloor was due essentially to sediment cover. In the areas that were smooth, the sediments were thick enough to obscure all of the major topographic features of the basement relief, whereas in the rough areas the sediments were insufficiently thick to disguise, in any major way, the essential relief of the basement beneath.

However, the nature of the seafloor and its origins remained less certain until I came across evidence of the Rift Valley.

These splatter cones are located on the Galapagos Islands, a volcanic island group lying west of Ecuador.

THE RIFT VALLEY

While Bruce Heezen was surveying the Mid-Atlantic Ridge with an echo sounder on the *Atlantis I*, I was interpreting the soundings he obtained and turning them into ocean profiles. One day I discovered a deep, V-shaped cleft at the crest of the ridge, which greatly intrigued me. It appeared as a line down the middle of the North Atlantic, parallel to the neighboring continents. When I showed Bruce my "discovery," he just groaned and said it looked too much like continental drift. I had to admit he was right. Although by now the Europeans had somewhat accepted Wegener's theory, in the United States of 1952, it was still tantamount to scientific heresy.

Pleurosicya boldinghi is one of about 2,000 species of gobies, small fishes that mainly inhabit the shallow waters of tropical and temperate zones. Gobies were in existence in the Eocene Period, 50 million years ago.

What is the connection between a mid-ocean valley and continental drift? If continental drift did exist, the valley I had noticed would have been formed by molten rock rising under the ridge crest and splitting it in two. This activity would gradually have carried the continental blocks apart.

It was around this time that Bruce and I decided to make a physiographic diagram of the North Atlantic. This was done in the style of A. K. Lobeck, then a professor of geomorphology at Columbia University. His physiographic diagrams of many countries were well known to geology students of the time and are still in use today. We chose this artistic and interpretive style because contour charts of the seafloor were classified by the U.S. Navy. With a physiographic diagram, it was possible to blur the actual position of topographic features. We continued with this style even after soundings were declassified in 1961 because we enjoyed working in this mode, demanding though it was.

Bruce did his master's thesis on the 1929 Grand Banks earthquake. In investigating submarine cable breaks caused by the earthquake, he confirmed the existence of turbidity currents in the deep sea and the great speeds they can attain. Upon publication of his thesis, Bruce was approached by Bell Laboratories and asked to determine where the utility should lay new transatlantic cables. His first approach to the problem was to plot the position of all known earthquakes. To do this, he used data from seismographs, devices that record the intensity of earth vibrations. However, compared with present-day methods for determining the location of epicenters, these early methods were highly inaccurate. A window of accuracy of up to three hundred miles (480 km) was considered usual, while today, five miles (8 km) is the norm. Bruce found the seismographic information inadequate in comparison with our data of the ocean floor.

While I was working on our physiographic diagram of the North Atlantic, I happened to notice a map lying on an adjoining table. This map, in the same scale as I was using, pictured the epicenters of shallow focus earthquakes. It appeared to me that the location of these earthquakes closely followed the central valley appearing on our map. Further research showed the epicenters fell within the valley itself.

Earthquakes, topographically speaking, may be expressed as a deep trench, valley, crack, escarpment or a high mountain range. These are the result of compression (forcing together), tension (moving apart) or shear (as in a strike-slip fault, where both horizontal and vertical movement is involved) in the Earth's crust. We wondered which of these forces had created our valley.

I incorporated the earthquakes into our physiographic diagram. With our newly discovered correlation, Bruce and I tracked our ridge valley around the globe following the earthquake epicenter belt. We were led up the Indian Ocean, through the Gulf of Aden, across the Afar Desert, and down through the Rift Valleys of East Africa. With our correlation of three parameters— earthquakes, ridge and rift valley—we were able to use quakes alone to trace our rift valley and ridge around the world for 40,000 miles (65,000 km). Eventually, it was determined that the rift valley averaged 10,000 feet (3,000 m) in depth and six to thirty miles (13 to 48 km) in width. In comparison, the Grand Canyon is on average 4,000 feet (1,200 m) deep, four to eighteen miles (6 to 29 km) wide and about two hundred miles (320 km) long.

In the process of tracing our ridge around the world, we picked up what had been considered isolated features, such as the Carlsberg Ridge in the Indian Ocean. During the late 1950s and early 1960s, data obtained from the voyage of the research vessel *Vema* confirmed that the ridge and the rift valley existed in several parts of the seafloor. It was the extension of the mid-oceanic ridge system into East Africa that finally convinced Bruce that our valley was real. We called it a rift valley because it was tensional in origin as are the African rift valleys.

In 1956, Bruce and Maurice Ewing presented a paper at an American Geophysical Union meeting in Toronto. This was the first public presentation hinting at the possibility of what Bruce would call "continental displacement"; it was still professional suicide to use the word "drift." In 1959, at the First International Oceanographic Congress in New York City, Bruce gave thirteen papers, including discussions of continental displacement and related subjects. At this meeting, Jacques Cousteau, the French marine explorer, made an unannounced appearance with a fascinating piece of film. Cousteau had seen

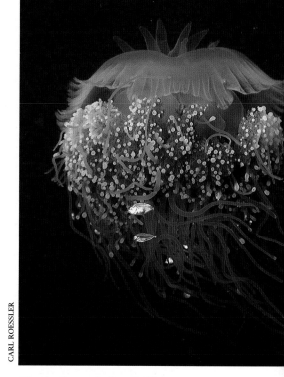

The fossil record of umbrella- or bell-shaped jellyfishes can be traced back to the Jurassic Period (190 to 160 million years ago) or, some believe, the Cambrian Period (570 to 515 million years ago).

A luminescent pink helmet jellyfish (Aglantha digitale) *from the Arctic feeds on plankton.*

our physiographic diagram of the North Atlantic but had not believed in the rift valley's existence. He had taken his vessel, the *Calypso*, with a sled, the *Troika*, in tow across the area where the valley was purported to be. A movie camera mounted on the sled took breathtaking footage of the black cliffs of the valley and convinced him that it did, in fact, exist.

After completing the physiographic diagram of the North Atlantic, I began another of the South Atlantic. Upon publication in 1961, it was difficult to avoid the evidence that continental drift existed, and now it has become a widely accepted concept. With the support of additional studies in paleoclimatology, paleontology and paleomagnetics, and the discovery of a lubricated layer deep in the Earth's crust for continents to drift upon, continental drift has evolved into the theory of plate tectonics — the idea that huge, rigid blocks, or plates, move about on an Earth which retains a constant volume. The plates are separated by mid-ocean ridges, deep-sea trenches, active mountain chains or fault zones. Plates move together, move apart or move past each other depending on the type of boundary separating them.

The Hawaiian Islands, a volcanic island chain, illustrate the movement of a plate westward. As one moves northwest along the chain, the islands become progressively older. Only the youngest island, Hawaii, has active volcanoes. The islands were produced one after the other over a long period of time as the Pacific plate moved over a "hot spot" of magma anchored in the asthenosphere. The "hot spot" is now located beneath the Kilauea crater on Hawaii, but eventually this island will also drift away and the magma will well up in another place and begin forming a new island.

The research into the origins of the sea and land continue. I, too, continue to map and write about the ocean floor, but today I know that the actual sea bottom looks much different than the one I mapped in the 1950s. It is littered with dangerous debris, and even the water itself contains chemicals that did not exist forty years ago. Let us hope that in this decade we will once again see the oceans as a place of discovery, rather than as a place to dump the unwanted refuse from our shores. Let us hope that we will learn to respect this ancient birthplace of all life before it is too late.

*The ancestors of the pearly nautilus (*Nautilus pompilius*), a relative of the octopus, cuttle-fish and squid, have lived in the ocean for hundreds of millions of years. These cephalopod mollusks are most often found in the Indian Ocean and the South Pacific.*

THE DIVERSITY OF LIFE IN THE OCEANS

Opposite:

The Red Irish Lord (Hemilepi-dotus hemilepidotus) *is susceptible to coastal pollution and dumping.*

Life in the oceans ranges from single-celled plants to complex multi-celled creatures. It is a highly diverse world. It is also a world that is not familiar to many of us. Even scientists are only beginning to understand the interrelationships of marine organisms, particularly of those that live in the open ocean. To conserve all forms of life at all levels, we need to learn much more about these interrelationships and the impact of human activities on them.

Above:

The slime coating on this anemone fish (Amphiprion sandaracinos) *helps protect it from the tentacles of its host.*

Above and right:

To those who are not familiar with sea anemones (order Actiniaria), it is sometimes a shock to find that they are not underwater flowers but carnivorous animals. Food caught by the animal's tentacles is passed to its mouth in the middle of the tentacle ring and sucked into its stomach.

Feather stars (order Comatulida) have one of the most primitive methods of food gathering in the animal kingdom. They wait in elevated areas with outstretched arms to capture plankton and tiny organisms drifting by in the currents.

Regal angelfish (Pygoplites dia-canthus) *swim among the coral reefs that line both coasts of the Red Sea. In areas close to major coastal towns, the extensive collection of corals and shells, and the damage caused by divers and boat anchors, are changing the reef environment.*

A school of golden sweepers (Parapriacanthus ransonneti). *Schooling in fish is associated with defense, feeding and repro-duction.*

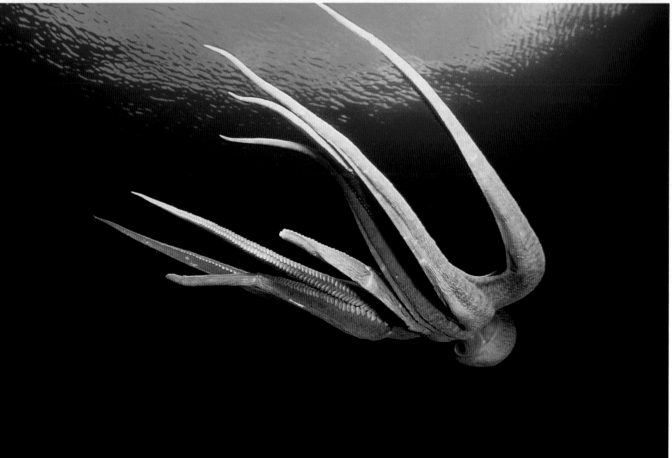

Above:

*The sunflower seastar (*Pycno-podia helianthoides*) of the North Pacific can grow to 3 feet (1 m) in diameter.*

Left:

*When the giant Pacific octopus (*Octopus dofleini*) is disturbed, its usual dull coloring changes to a rosy hue. This large cephalopod can weigh up to 100 pounds (45 kg).*

Opposite:

*Octopus (*Octopus dofleini*) eye. Unlike many other sea creatures, the octopus relies on its eyesight to recognize its prey.*

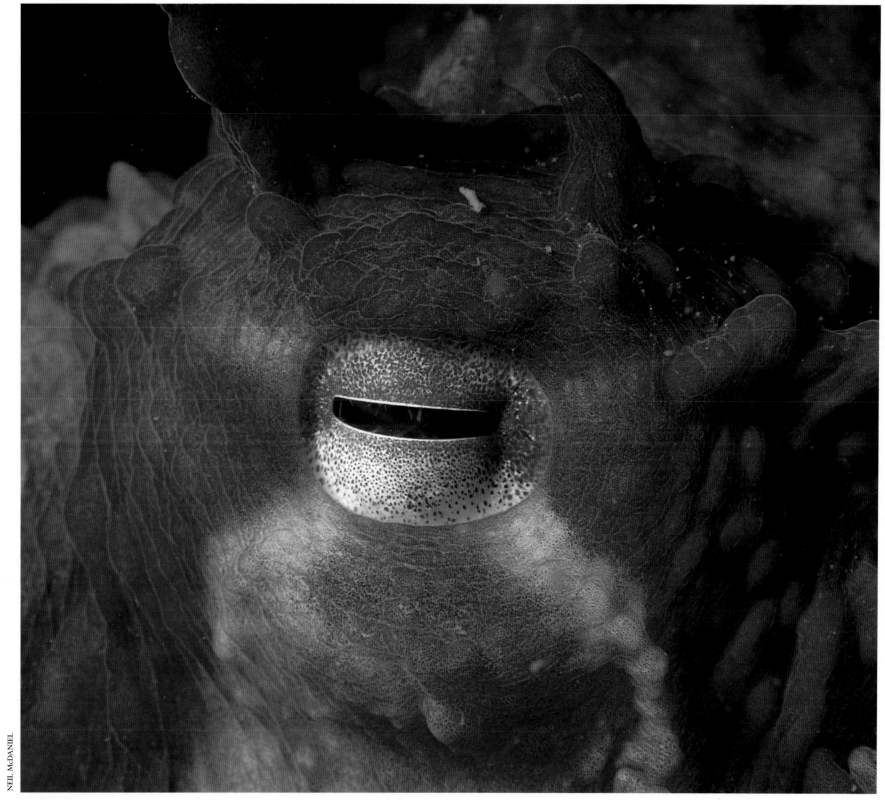

THE PLANET'S LIFEBELT

T. R. PARSONS

NO BEING WHO HAS VIEWED THIS PLANET FROM SPACE WOULD christen it "Earth." The term reflects our unfamiliarity with the extent and importance of the global ocean, as well as our anthropocentric viewpoint. If our planet is listed in any extraterrestrial encyclopedia of planets and stars, then surely it is named for its dominant feature—a vast expanse of blue water. Ten times the volume of our land mass could be buried below its surface.

It is fortunate that the large sink of the oceans is in great volumetric disproportion to the land. This has enabled the sea to absorb the tremendous geological upheavals of undersea volcanic activity, as well as much of the terrestrial debris. The resilience of the oceans has been an ecological blessing. At the same time, the oceans produce an amount of plant and animal life approximately equivalent to that found on the land. Thus, from ancient times, the seas have been a benevolent source of food for humans.

It is difficult for many of us to envision the biological complexity of the marine environment. All the marine plants and most of the animals live in the upper 3,300 feet (1,000 m) of the oceans. Life is believed to have begun in the sea, and even today there are marine animal species that have never evolved terrestrial counterparts. Some of these ocean residents have a very long evolutionary history; jellyfish and corals, for example, were living in the sea at least 500 million years ago. Fish appeared approximately 350 million years ago, while whales are newcomers to the ocean, having moved into the marine environment from the land only about 60 million years ago.

Opposite:

Fishing boats in Bergen, Norway. The removal of vast quantities of fish every year by the world's fishing nations represents the single greatest impact on ocean ecology by people.

Sea cucumbers (class Holothu-roidea) ingest sediments from the sea bottom to obtain food. Some species are harvested and dried for sale as a food product in the Far East. The effect of this harvest on populations is not known, because there has been little resource assessment, especially in tropical fisheries.

Some of the animals that have been around longest may be the most adaptable to environmental change because, throughout their history, the ocean has been subjected to enormous geophysical and astrophysical forces. Today, the seas and their inhabitants are undergoing ever-increasing change caused by the impact of a rapidly expanding human population that produces large quantities of waste products and that has the ability to manufacture synthetic chemicals, the likes of which have never been encountered in the 500-million-year evolution of marine organisms. Humans can now create ecological impacts on a global scale, and this raises fundamental questions about the durability of life in the sea. It is high time to ask, "What exactly are we doing to the oceans?"

It is possible that even a million years ago, the first primitive humans harvested food from the sea and traveled short distances over its surface by boat. Historical evidence of seafaring peoples can be surmised from the spread of civilizations over several thousand years. By the time of Aristotle (384-322 B.C.), there was already at least a commercial interest in naming the different fish of the sea. Modern oceanographic studies date from 1872, with the circumnavigation of the HMS *Challenger*, a British ship commissioned specially to explore the ocean depths. It has only been in the last 150 years that we have been in any position to determine how we are affecting the ecology of the seas.

A wide range of human activities affect the oceans. Some activities have an impact on the whole ocean system. The effect of other activities is more localized, with the degree of disturbance diminishing with distance from the source of the impact. The nature of the impact depends, too, on the type and concentration of substances introduced into the sea. If large amounts of a chemical such as petroleum are introduced from a tanker, the impact is called pollution. However petroleum is a natural substance that seeps into marine habitats in many places in the world, including off the coast of Santa Barbara, California. A specialized marine community has evolved to live in these natural petroleum sites. On the other hand, many synthetic chemicals (for example, PCBs) have no natural marine counterparts.

Too often, human activities that influence ocean ecology are viewed from

an anthropocentric philosophy. Those activities that are regarded as beneficial to humans are ignored as having potentially devastating effects on marine life. For example, the fishing industry certainly kills far more fish than any pollutant, yet there has never been an environmental impact statement about the effect of fish harvesting on ocean ecology.

The harvesting of resources and the introduction into the sea of certain pollutants are large-scale impacts that affect the entire ocean system. With respect to these activities, we are most definitely affecting the ecology of the seas.

The low reproductive rate of the dugong (Dugong dugon)*, a relative of the manatee, makes it particularly vulnerable to extinction by overhunting and other man-made threats.*

THE HARVESTING OF MARINE RESOURCES

Humans have harvested some marine creatures to extinction. One example is the Steller's sea cow (*Hydrodamalis gigas*). This large relative of the manatee and the dugong was discovered in 1741, when a Russian vessel under the

MUSSELS

BARNACLES

SEAWEED

CRAB

CORALS

SHRIMP

SEA ANEMONE

GIANT CLAM

SEAHORSES

SEA URCHINS

STARFISH

SPONGE

SCALLOPS

FEATHER STAR

MARINE WORMS

SEA CUCUMBER

SPONGES

GULLS

BUTTERFLY FISH

JELLYFISH

SEAL

SALMON

OCTOPUS

HOGFISH

LEATHERBACK TURTLE

NAUTILUS

SQUID

SWALLOWER

DEEPSEA SMELTS

SNIPE EEL

CRINOIDS

DEEPSEA SKATE

BRITTLE STAR

Not drawn to scale.

DISTRIBUTION OF
MARINE LIFE
IN THE OCEAN

ZOOPLANKTON

PHYTOPLANKTON

FLYING FISH

DOLPHINS

SUNLIT ZONE
650 FEET (200 M)

TWILIGHT ZONE
3,300 FEET (1,000 M)

HERRING

BELUGA WHALE

TUNA

SHARK

MARLIN

SALPS

LANTERNFISH

BATHYPELAGIC ZONE
13,100 FEET (4,000 M)

SPERM WHALE

HATCHETFISH

ABYSSOPELAGIC ZONE

ANGLERFISH

RATFISH

GULPER

DEEP SEA VENT

CRABS

TUBE WORMS

VENUS' FLOWER BASKET

Manatees (Trichechus mana-
tus), plant-eating tropical
mammals, are threatened by
overhunting, outboard motor
propellers, pollution, entangle-
ment in fishing gear and loss of
habitat.

command of Captain Vitus Bering was wrecked on the remote Commander Islands in the subarctic North Pacific. As described by George Steller, the ship's naturalist, the sea cows were docile, slow-moving mammals that lived in shallow water and grazed on massive kelp forests. The survivors of the shipwreck were not long in discovering that this huge, gentle creature was easily killed. It had no form of self-defense other than its immense weight of ten tons. Author Delphine Haley gives the following eyewitness description of the capture of a Steller's sea cow:

> One could safely row a boat into the midst of a herd while the animals grazed with heads underwater. After a few unsuccessful attempts, they hooked a sea cow from a boat and pulled it in by rope, a feature requiring the efforts of forty men on land. En route the beast struggled and sighed; some other sea cows tried to rescue the captive by pressing on the rope and upsetting the boat with their backs. Once landed, the immense animal was hewn and carved into sections. The resulting sea cow steaks were described as "exceedingly savory"; even more delicious to the malnourished crew was the fat, which tasted like sweet almond-oil.

Unfortunately, the sea cow tasted much better than the seals and otters on which the starving crew would have otherwise had to depend for their survival. The rescued survivors carried back word about the delightful feast of sea cow that could be had on the Commander Islands, and this report quickly spread to other Russian vessels engaged in the Alaskan fur trade. The fate of the species was sealed.

In 1741, there were thought to be about two thousand sea cows on the Commander Islands. This was, however, the last remaining population of these animals, which once ranged all the way from California to the coast of Japan. Their gentle nature had probably attracted the attention of prehistoric humans, and their elimination from all previous habitats would not have been difficult for even the most primitive hunters. By 1768, only twenty-seven years after their discovery, the last member of the last population of the Steller's sea cow had been killed and eaten.

Today, the closely related manatees (*Trichechus manatus*) of the tropical Atlantic have been severely depleted through hunting and loss of habitat. However, in some areas, their chances of survival have been increased by habitat protection programs and bans on harvesting. Less assurance can be given for the Indo-Pacific dugongs (*Dugong dugon*), which continue to be harvested by local inhabitants in need of a rich source of protein.

The flightless great auk (*Pinguinus impennis*) of the North Atlantic Ocean was also eliminated by humans. This bird was the original "penguin"; its name was given much later to the flightless birds of the southern hemisphere. A number of "Penguin Islands" still exist off Newfoundland, where the great auk might have been seen by early travelers in the sixteenth and seventeenth centuries. The principal nesting colony of this very large bird—it was almost two feet (60 cm) in height—was on remote Funk Island, off the northeastern tip of Newfoundland. Eighteenth-century seafarers came to this locale to harvest the bird for its soft, downy feathers, as well as for meat when needed. There was no fuel on the island and so the giant auks were also burned; their thick layer of fat helped to ignite the fires in which other birds were scalded to remove their feathers. Author Ralph Whitlock gives the following account of what was believed to be the demise of the last of the great auks, killed on the Scottish island of St. Kilda in 1840:

> A party of five men visiting the outlying Stac an Armin surprised one asleep on a ledge, secured it by tying its legs and kept it alive for three days. On the third day a storm blew up, and the men, fearing that the bird was a witch responsible for the gale, beat it to death with sticks.

Today a similar fate may await some marine turtles, which are harvested for food (both meat and eggs), for their shells and for use in fertility potions. At one South China Sea site on the east coast of Malaysia, the number of leatherback turtle (*Dermochelys coriacea*) nests declined from nearly two thousand in the 1950s to fewer than one hundred in the 1980s. Whereas the leatherback turtle does nest in other areas and is not now classified as an endangered species, other species are declining rapidly. The hawksbill turtle (*Eretmochelys imbricata*), for example, is highly prized for its beautiful shell, which is the true tortoiseshell of commerce. This animal is severely threatened by harvesting in southeast Asia, where its sale boosts the fortunes of local inhabitants. The green turtle (*Chelonia midas*), formerly an abundant species, is the main ingredient for turtle soup. Because their restricted nesting sites have become easily accessible to humans, all marine turtle populations can be regarded as endangered. In some areas, however, the limited numbers of

hawksbill, green and leatherback turtles are officially classified as "endangered species" by the International Union for the Conservation of Nature (IUCN).

A rather different situation regarding the protection of a marine species occurred recently with respect to the Canadian harp seal (*Phoca groenlandica*) harvest. Harp seals are the second most abundant seal in the world. The three populations that breed in the Gulf of St. Lawrence, on an island off Greenland and in the White Sea off the Siberian coast probably number over 4 million. Despite its not being an endangered species, a concerted effort to prevent the killing of the young seal pups by environmental groups in the 1960s was successful in closing down this harvest. The primary motive for ending the hunt was not related to conservation; it was the innocent appeal of the pups faced with the brutality of the seal hunt that aroused public sympathy and forced a ban on the harvest.

The slaughter of young harp seals (Phoca groenlandica) *for their fur aroused worldwide public indignation in the 1960s and resulted in a ban on their harvest in the Gulf of St. Lawrence.*

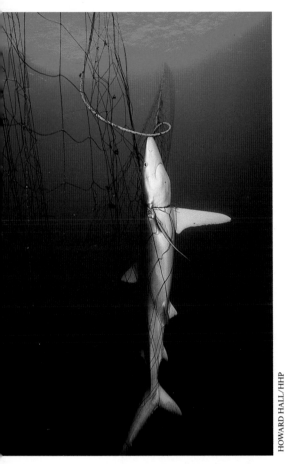

Many unmarketable species are caught in fishing nets and discarded at sea. The blue shark (Prionace glauca) has been considered a nuisance by fishermen for centuries because it damages nets and lines. However, as the stocks of traditional fish, such as haddock and cod, decline in the northern Atlantic, it has recently become a fishing target itself.

Perhaps the greatest impact of humans on ocean ecology is not by harvesting any one particular species, but by the removal of 90 million tons of fish per year by the world's fishing nations. This is the statistic published by the Food and Agricultural Organization (FAO) of the United Nations. This figure represents only the reported catch of the commercially important species. Those unwanted, unmarketable species that are caught by the indiscriminate fishing of bottom trawls, purse seines and driftnets are usually discarded at sea and are not counted as "catch." They include large quantities of unmarketable fish, as well as marine mammals and birds. For example, several hundred thousand seabirds may be killed annually in driftnets that are set primarily for squid; this is a significant mortality rate, even for some species of marine bird populations which may number in the tens of millions. Similarly, in the purse-seine tuna fishery, millions of dolphins are believed to have been killed since the 1970s. Recently, this fishery has been brought under some control by requiring fishermen to use a redesigned tuna net that allows the dolphins to escape. Also unreported and uncounted are the many bottom-dwelling creatures (including turtles) captured in shrimp trawls, and the discarding of sharks after collection of their fins, which are used in shark's fin soup. Taken together, the unreported and uncounted biomass removed from the ocean would probably be at least equal to the reported catch, making a total mortality of marine creatures of about 200 million tons per year. This is variously estimated to represent between 20 percent and 50 percent of the potential total harvestable fish in the oceans.

Furthermore, because it is often easier to capture the larger fish, many of the species that are harvested are top-level predators in the marine food chain. Ecologically, this is similar to removing the lions from the plains of Africa, an action that would surely result in a population explosion of antelopes and a decimation of vegetation. The ocean may work in a similar way, or it may have its own response. In any event, there is no form of pollution that has the large-scale impact of this one industry.

In the 1970s, the largest fishery in the world was the anchovy fishery off the coast of Peru. The total harvest in 1970 reached 12 million tons. Ocean climate changes coupled with such heavy fishing pressure led to the collapse

Krill (Euphausia superba*) is the mainstay of the Southern Ocean food chain.*

of the anchovy population, and the harvest now amounts to only 2 or 3 million tons. In retrospect we may ask, "What happened to the ecology of the area when 12 million tons of anchovy were removed in a single year?" No specific studies were conducted to answer this question, but we do know that about 10 million seabirds that had once fed on the anchovy disappeared at the same time. In addition, much of the phytoplankton on which the adult anchovy fed was not grazed and simply sank out of the water column to form an anoxic sediment on the seafloor.

The problems of overfishing are sometimes compounded by wasteful use of the resource. Much of the Peruvian anchovy harvest was turned into chicken feed, as is the case in the present-day 5-million-ton Chilean sardine fishery. This practice is a waste of high-quality animal protein that could be consumed directly by humans. However, the economics of the world food supply make fish more valuable as poultry feed in America than as human food in Africa or Asia, where it is needed most.

Today, the largest fishery in the world is the Alaskan walleye pollock (*Theragra chalcogramma*) fishery in the Bering Sea. In 1986, its harvest was about 6.6 million tons. Recent studies have indicated that the annual removal of this amount of fish has caused decreases in a number of other animal populations that depend on pollock, including sea lions, fur seals and some marine birds such as murres. Other marine birds (for example, the auklet) that feed on zooplankton, the food of the pollock, have increased in number because their food has presumably become more abundant with the removal of so much pollock.

Another documented change in ocean ecology is found in the Antarctic, where hunting has reduced the blue-whale (*Balaenoptera musculus*) population from about 228,000 to a present-day population of about 14,000. This has led to a ten-fold increase in the population of crabeater seals (*Lobodon carcinophagus*), a five-fold increase in minke whales (*Balaenoptera acutorostrata*) and an equivalent increase in some penguin species. All of these animals, like the decimated blue whales, feed on the shrimplike krill, which became more available to other animals following intensive whaling. Now the superabundant krill are becoming a commercial fishery target themselves. If these are

Gray reef sharks (Carcharhinus amblyrhynchos)*, Minto Reef, Micronesia. Sharks were once considered trash fish, but shark's fin soup is a fashionable delicacy, particularly in the Orient, and has made these fish a desirable catch. Only the fins are saved.*

The ocean floor after the destruction of a once lush kelp forest by a sea urchin (class Echinoidea) population explosion.

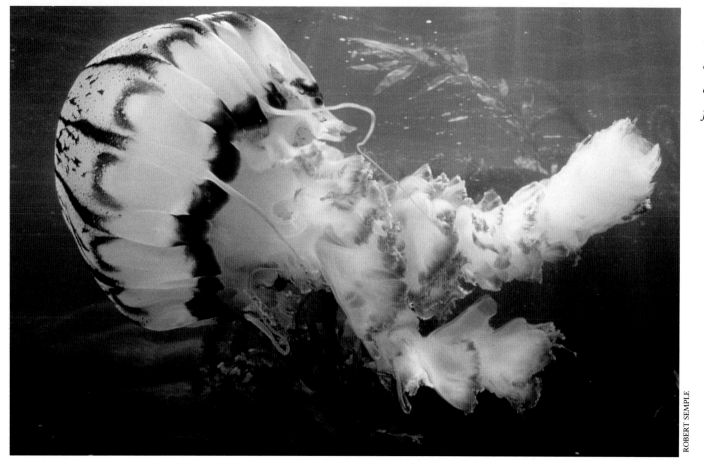

The purple striped jellyfish (Pelagia colorata) lives off the coast of California. Jellyfishes are ancient competitors with fish for food.

depleted, it is unlikely that the blue-whale population will ever return to its former levels.

As the world's fisheries continue to expand, other changes in ocean ecology are becoming apparent. For example, there were formerly twenty-six species of commercial fish in the Black Sea; now only five species are fished commercially. An added disturbance in this rather confined marine habitat is that there are now huge populations of jellyfish, a phenomenon that has also been recorded in the intensively fished North Sea. Could the removal of fish from the sea result in massive increases in the number of jellyfish? These invertebrate animals are, after all, the more ancient competitors with fish for zooplankton food. Thus one effect of humans on the oceans could be to cause a reversal in the evolution of marine food chains. There are some scientific grounds to support such a hypothesis, but at present the answer remains unknown.

Fisheries that target invertebrate animals (as opposed to fish) may also disrupt ecological patterns and set up irreversible changes. The American lobster (*Homarus americanus*) forms the basis for a lucrative fishery along the eastern North American seaboard. Some studies suggest that the removal of tons of lobsters from the area has caused an explosion in the population of spiny sea urchins (*Strongylocentrotus droebachiensis*), one of the lobsters' prey. As a result, the urchins eat all the seaweed beds, which are a natural protective cover for young lobsters. Thus, a potentially irreversible cycle is begun in which the overharvesting of lobsters destroys the very habitat in which they live.

Unfortunately, it is only in hindsight that we have discovered the disruptive effects of overharvesting. The most intensive studies of marine harvesting have been supported by fishing companies and have been directed toward methods that will allow them to continue to catch more fish, more efficiently. However, the fishing companies need to understand that their activities are disrupting the ecology of the oceans. Just as the logging industry should be held responsible for maintaining the ecology of our forests, the fishing industry should be held responsible for an ecologically rational exploitation of our oceans.

© NORBERT WU 1991

*The thousands of known sponge species live from coastal waters to the abyss. This vase sponge (*Callyspongia plicifera*) filters water for plankton off the Netherlands Antilles in the Caribbean. The development of synthetic bath sponges has all but ended the sponge fishing industry.*

*Studies suggest that the removal of tons of American lobsters (*Homarus americanus*) from the eastern North American seaboard has caused the population of its principal prey, the spiny sea urchin (*Strongylocentrotus droebachiensis*), to increase dramatically.*

ROBERT SEMPLE

THE IMPACT OF POLLUTANTS

Burning of fossil fuels is causing an accumulation of carbon dioxide in the atmosphere at a rate that will double the concentration by the year 2050. Projected consequences include a global warming of as much as 5°C (41°F) in some places, elevations in sea level ranging from eight inches to seven feet (20 cm to 2 m), and increased coastal winds and precipitation. Much of the increase in carbon dioxide in the atmosphere may be absorbed by the oceans. This is not of particular concern to ocean ecology because the oceans already contain sixty times more carbon dioxide than the atmosphere. However, global warming will affect the seas. Elevated seawater temperatures may alter migration patterns of fish stocks, affect the survival of fish larvae living at boundaries between cold and warm water and change the quantity of plankton in some areas. In the latter case, since plankton form the basis for practically all marine life, any dramatic change in abundance could affect the entire food chain.

A Pacific squid fishery illustrates how seawater temperatures can change ocean ecology in a particular area. The squid appear in waters off the coast of Washington State whenever there is an intrusion of warm water into the area. The arrival of the squid is accompanied by an increase in the number of tuna, but by a decrease in some of the more southerly salmon stocks.

Other hydrospheric impacts can be detected by the widespread occurrence of airborne pesticides in marine organisms. DDT remains the best example of this, although, due to the decreased use of this chemical, the problem has abated since the 1970s. Hydrospheric contamination in all such cases results from pesticides being sprayed onto land, where some particles are picked up in the atmosphere and carried considerable distances before being deposited again in precipitation. Japanese scientists showed that DDT that had been used in southeast Asia was carried as far as Antarctic waters, occurring at the surface in concentrations of about 0.1 parts per billion. DDT has also been detected in Antarctic animals which, of course, have never been directly subjected to this pesticide.

A major problem with synthetic chemicals like DDT is that they are new to nature in an evolutionary sense. One can never predict exactly how organisms or communities will react to a new poison, even if present in tiny amounts, because they have never experienced this particular condition, nor built any resistance to it, during their millions of years of evolution. Although evolutionary history has included adaptation to poisonous chemicals—many plants contain toxic chemicals that deter animals from eating them — the timespan of such evolutionary events has been slow compared to the accelerated pace of human intervention.

Today we only understand, for the most part, the acute effects of pollutants in the oceans. Chronic effects may take much longer to diagnose. For example, petroleum is generally present in surface waters at concentrations of a few milligrams per meter squared. The oil floats mostly as tar lumps, which in turn are colonized as habitats for drifting barnacles and seaweeds. Although this is an unnatural condition, in a short time frame this form of pollution might seem more beneficial to the colonizing species than harmful. Pieces of plastic and commercial lumber may also be colonized at sea by plants and animals. Much more hazardous, and completely invisible, is the potential for open ocean contamination by radioactive materials. Eight nuclear reactors in

© NORBERT WU 1991

*Brown pelicans (*Pelecanus occidentalis*) are making a comeback after their numbers were decimated by DDT contamination.*

*A sea butterfly (family Clioni-
dae) uses its winglike parts to
swim through the surface waters
of the North Atlantic. Like the
nudibranch, it is a snail without a shell.*

submarines are lying on the ocean floor waiting to disintegrate and release their deadly cargo. French nuclear tests on the Pacific atoll of Mururoa are not considered by some scientists to be safe against eventual leakage of radioactive wastes from the atoll. Since some of these radioactive chemicals are active for thousands of years, the dangers remain.

"Red tides" represent another hydrospheric problem that occurs mainly along tropical and temperate coasts. The term describes a reddish discoloration of seawater caused by one of several marine microorganisms. Some of these red-tide organisms are completely harmless, but others contain a potent toxin that can be accumulated by the shellfish that feed on the red-tide species. The shellfish are not harmed, but their accumulated toxin is powerful enough to kill any vertebrate, including people who eat the contaminated oysters or clams. The poisoning in humans is referred to as paralytic shellfish poisoning (PSP). This is not a new phenomenon. One of the earliest records of PSP was in 1793, when one death and four illnesses resulted from crew members on Captain George Vancouver's ship eating toxic mussels off the west coast of Canada. In 1799, one hundred men on a Russian expedition off Alaska died from eating mussels.

The incidence of red tides is growing, and there is no obvious explanation except a suspicion that it may be caused by increasing amounts of nutrients from agriculture and sewage being released in coastal zones. There are now widespread programs for the testing of all shellfish products; if any contain a trace of the toxin, the shallow water area from which the shellfish were taken is closed to further harvesting. Usually contaminated shellfish purge them-selves of the toxin, and repeated testing allows for their eventual harvest.

THE FUTURE OF THE OCEAN HABITAT

The oceans are so enormous relative to land areas that it is sometimes difficult to imagine that humans could have any lasting impact on them. Most people only see the ocean margins, and it is here that they glimpse the effects of our industrial society on marine ecology. There are far more examples of human

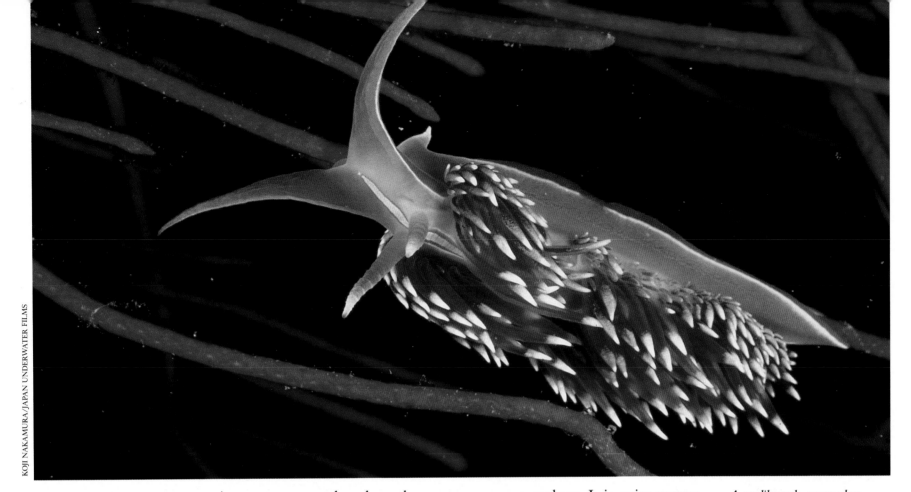

impacts on coastal ecology than on open-ocean ecology. It is quite correct, therefore, to focus our attention and concern on these areas, whether they are the polar ice shelves or tropical mangrove forests. Many of these continental and island margins have suffered from some form of exploitation. However, pollution or destruction in these areas can often be readily corrected through better management. The secret to success is to view coastal zones not primarily as areas of development, but as places where humans must learn to live in harmony with the sea. Concepts of anthropocentric greed must give way to ecocentric need. High-density development must be replaced with low-density envelopment, retaining natural coastal habitats as part of low-density human habitats.

The case for protecting the open ocean is quite different. Humans have had far less impact on open-ocean ecology than along coasts. Furthermore, it is almost impossible to do very much about such vast areas that are influenced much more by the world climate than by humans. Nevertheless, with respect to high-seas fisheries, global warming and atmospheric pollutants, it is certainly possible to curtail some of the excesses that our human economy has produced.

A nudibranch, or sea slug (order Nudibranchia), is a shell-less marine snail that lives in shallow water.

THE TWILIGHT ZONE

SYLVIA EARLE

BLUE LIGHTS DANCE AND FLASH AGAINST A FIELD OF DEEPEST INDIGO . . . a dozen slender gray forms streak by in close formation . . . something silver shimmers in the distance. Above, the sea appears faintly blue; below, the blackest black imaginable, and all around the aura of that time and space between light and darkness — the twilight zone.

Only a small fraction of the sea is illuminated. That liquid realm, home for more than 90 percent of life on Earth, is mostly dark all of the time, and all of it is dark at least some of the time.

Like light, heat is concentrated near the surface of the sea. Even in the tropics, the temperature 1,000 feet (300 m) down may be near freezing. Pressure is another factor that powerfully influences living conditions with increasing depth. At the sea surface, the weight of the fifteen or so miles (24 km) of air above creates an overall 14.7 pounds (6.6 kg) of weight per square inch. Only thirty-three feet (10 m) of seawater creates an equivalent amount of weight or "one atmosphere." Creatures living at 1,000 feet (300 m) have the weight of about thirty-one atmospheres or 455 pounds (206 kg) pressing on each square inch of their bodies. Many, migrating vertically during day-night cycles of light, are subjected to pressure-change stresses far beyond anything experienced by even the highest-flying birds and insects or high-altitude balloonists. Humans venture here inside submersibles on strictly limited passports, or go vicariously, gingerly flying underwater robots from distant surface craft.

Opposite:

A pair of rays (Mobula) tandem swimming. Like sharks, rays have skeletons composed of cartilage rather than bone. Most live on or near the ocean floor feeding on bottom-dwellers, such as worms, shellfish and fish.

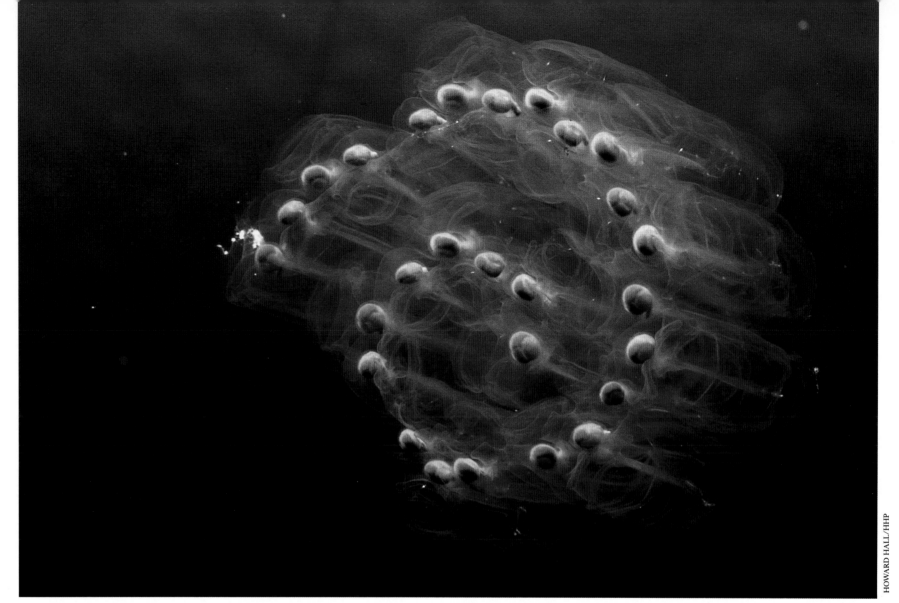

HOWARD HALL/HHP

Salps (class Thaliacea) are free-swimming, transparent organisms that live in colonies, as this one, or alone. For the most part, they inhabit warm seas.

Given a chance to dive beyond 1,000 feet (300 m) in a personal submersible, a one-man (or woman) hard-shell diving suit that eliminates the need for decompression, and given a chance to explore directly a part of the ocean that I had known only from crumpled samples snared in nets and smudged images on depth-sounding charts, what could I say? I said yes, of course. That's why, in 1979, I found myself watching the sunlit surface disappear in a froth of blue bubbles as I began my deepest dive to date, an excursion into the twilight zone six miles (10 km) offshore from Makapuu Point, Oahu, Hawaii, 1,250 feet (380 m) down.

There are no words to describe the blueness. I struggle with inadequate adjectives such as "translucent," "luminous," "ethereal," then surrender to the simple joy of experiencing the otherworldly quality of that blue-blue ocean space.

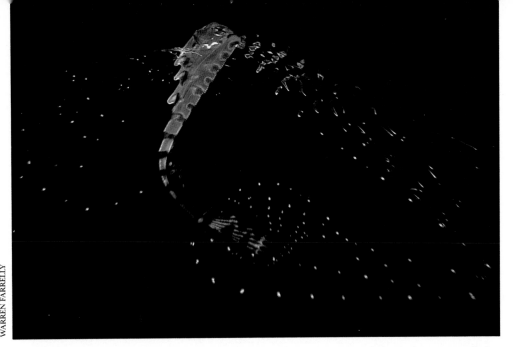

This juvenile ribbonfish (Zu) lives in the twilight zone. Its fin rays act as flotation devices and are thought by some scientists to mimic the siphonophore's stinging tentacles.

Part of the reason for making the dive was to evaluate the use of the diving system for potential research applications. Named "Jim" after Jim Jarrett, the first person willing to try an early version of the system in the late 1920s, the suit was designed for salvage operations and oil-field work—and for occupants significantly larger than I. The oil-filled joints that make up Jim's arms and legs require frequent flexing to prevent "freezing" under increasing pressure. It would be easier to do this, I keep thinking, if my arms reached the ends of the metal "sleeves." I lean first one way, then the other, to reach the ends of the mechanical arms.

"Jim" is normally deployed using a tether, connecting the system to a surface winch, which is used to reel the 1,000-pound (450-kg) suit in and out of the water. This time, the University of Hawaii's small two-man submarine, *Star II*, is used as an underwater taxi. Jim, with me inside, stands on a small platform jutting from the front of the sub. A band holds the suit in place until released by those inside *Star II*—the pilot, Bohdan Bartko, and cameraman Al Giddings. There is no cable to the surface, but a slender communication line extends between the sub and Jim.

Preoccupied with suit-mechanics and communicating with Bo and Al, who keep inquiring about my condition, I am disconcerted to find that I am at five hundred feet (150 m) and have not recorded anything in the notebook propped near my waist. Chains of crystalline salps, glistening spheres of small jelly-creatures, iridescent flecks of life, glide by the ports surrounding my face. And the incredible, glowing light! The blue gives way to blue-black, then black-blue, then near-darkness. At 1,000 feet (300 m), constellations of small,

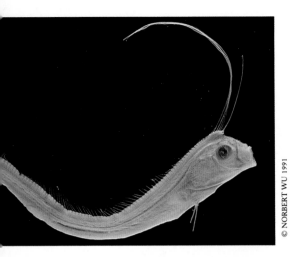

*The seldom seen oarfish (Rega-
lecus glesne) is the longest of
the bony fishes — up to 26 feet
(8 m) long. Its great length has
inspired many of the sea serpent
legends.*

luminous creatures brush against the suit, and at 1,150 feet (350 m), a faint image comes into focus below — the bottom.

Bo drives the sub to deeper water and parks amid a field of tall, slender bamboo coral, stately creatures that resemble giant curling whiskers, or enormous bedsprings sprouting from the seafloor. I am released from the sub's platform, and for two and a half glorious hours prowl the seafloor. The sub's lights illuminate a small patch of pink coral that is host to about a dozen red galatheid crabs. A lanternfish glides by, lights glowing like a miniature ocean liner. A large crab moves in and out of the illuminated area, clutching a small bouquet of coral in each of its two hindmost legs. "Why?" I muse. "What is that crab going to do with the coral?" There is no answer, just more questions. I touch one of the curling spirals of bamboo coral and watch rings of blue fire pulse from the tip to the bottom, and from the bottom back to the tip.

Curious about whether it might be possible to see without the sub's lights, I ask Bo and Al to please turn them off — then wait. My eyes gradually adjust to a scene reminiscent of that time just before dawn, that moment just past sunset, that time when stars are bright but there is no moon . . . when owls hoot, crickets chirp, coyotes howl. Here, small fish sparkle, red shrimp majestically glide by, and the glow of that elusive deep twilight blue prevails. Creatures for whom this place is home move in and out of my view, some as pale shadows, some glistening with small spangles of cold blue fire. Above, a midday sun warms the surface crew; on the seafloor below, I savor the last moments of a brief encounter with creatures that live at the edge of darkness.

THE EDGE OF DARKNESS

The amount of light reaching the sea surface depends on the time of day, season, latitude, cloud cover and other weather conditions. Once at the surface, light is modified at the air-sea interface by reflection and refraction, and both are affected by surface roughness — waves and ripples — or the presence of ice. A glassful of seawater appears clear, but every drop is likely

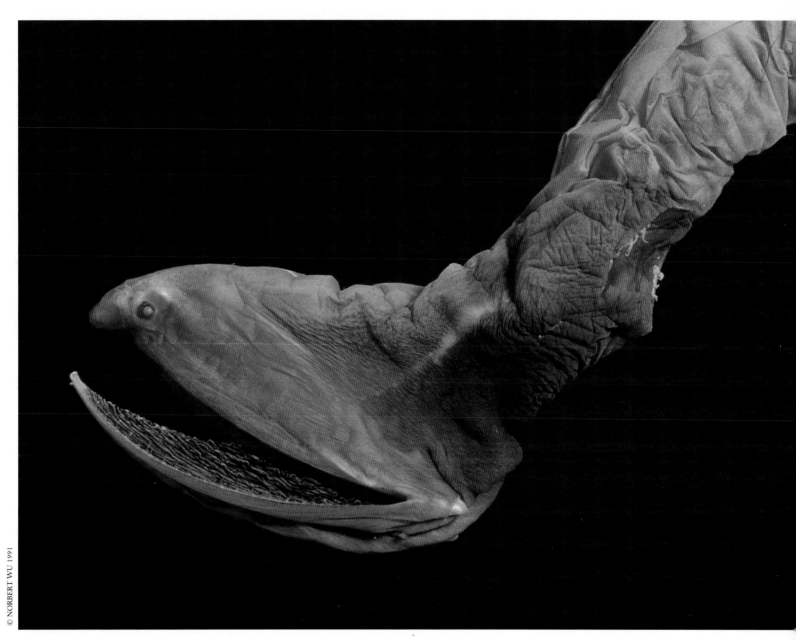

to contain inorganic particles and organic material, including minute living creatures that scatter, reflect, absorb and diffuse light that strikes the sea from above.

The depth where the transition zone between darkness and light occurs varies. In waters offshore from San Francisco or Hong Kong or Halifax, where the sea is often green-brown with plankton, silt and the mixed cargo that comes with proximity to urban areas, light diminishes rapidly within a

The gulper (Saccopharynx) is aptly named. It has an enormous mouth compared to its small body.

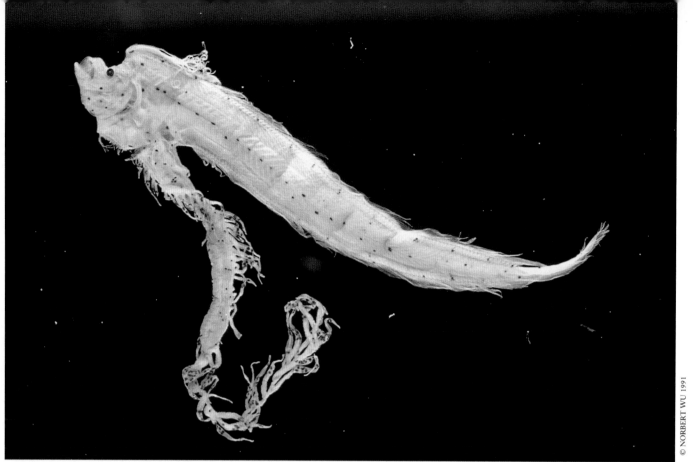

Many marine creatures have a larval stage in their life cycles. Because they often differ greatly in appearance from their adult form, a great number of larvae have yet to be identified. This one has been tentatively assigned to the Neobythitinae or cusk-eels, fishes that range from shallow to deep water.

few feet of the surface. In such areas, more than half the light striking the surface is extinguished at seven feet (2 m) depth; by twenty-six feet (8 m), more than 90 percent is gone. In the clearest ocean water at midday, sunlight may penetrate many times deeper than in turbid inshore areas, but in general, the intensity falls one tenth for about every 230 to 250 feet (70 to 75 m) increase in depth. Thus at 2,300 feet (700 m), the intensity is approximately a ten billionth of that at the surface. Even so, in a clear, open sea environment, light may be visible to a human observer at depths below 1,600 feet (500 m). For many creatures adapted for life at the edge of light — some with greatly modified eyes and special light-gathering pigments — light from the surface may be perceived at even greater depths. Some deep-sea fish and squid are thought to have light-sensing capability as much as one hundred times greater than that of humans.

It would seem simple to determine a maximum depth in the ocean where light fades and true darkness begins, but there are complicating factors beyond the obvious daily and seasonal differences in the amount of light that reaches the sea surface. Light from the sun is composed of different colors, corresponding to various wavelengths that appear white when mixed together. The longest rays — red, orange and yellow — are absorbed more quickly than the shorter blue, violet and green parts of the spectrum. Just under the surface, the full spectrum of visible light can be readily perceived, but even in the clearest ocean, orange, yellow and red are absorbed within the upper sixty-five feet (20 m). The realm below is characteristically blue.

Scientist and explorer William Beebe and engineer Otis Barton were the first to descend through the illuminated blue depths to the twilight zone and beyond. In his book, *Half Mile Down*, Beebe relates his impressions of the light observed through the tiny porthole of his two-man bathysphere during a dive near Bermuda in 1934:

> The sun was blazing over the oceans, the surface unusually quiet . . . down we slipped through the water. . . . the first plunge erases, to the eye, all the comforting, warm rays of the spectrum. The red and the orange are as if they have never been, and soon the yellow is swallowed up in the green. . . . The green faded imperceptibly as we went down, and at 200 feet it was impossible to say whether the water was greenish-blue or bluish-green. . . . At 600 feet the color appeared to be a dark, luminous blue, and this contradiction of terms shows the difficulty of description. At 1,000 feet . . . I tried to name the water; blackish-blue, dark gray-blue. The last hint of blue tapers into a nameless gray, and this finally into black. . . . At 1,900 feet, to my surprise, there was still the faintest hint of dead gray light, 200 feet deeper than usual, attesting to the almost complete calm of the surface and the extreme brilliance of the day far overhead. At 2,000 feet the world was forever black.

Forever black, perhaps, but studded with galaxies of living light, sparkling and glowing in thousands of variations. Throughout the sea, from the surface to the greatest depths, creatures flash with blue, green, yellow, orange and sometimes red light that emanates from special organs or from individual cells or tissues or in puffs of exuded, luminous liquid. Some 80 percent of sea creatures are thought to have some form of bioluminescence. It is an important, even vital aspect of life in the ocean, with some special adaptive twists for those living in the twilight zone.

Considerably more is known about the "hows" of bioluminescence than the "whys," although some fine speculations have been forthcoming about the strategies developed by creatures during hundreds of millions of years of sea history. At least seventeen chemical pathways produce light in creatures ranging from bacteria and single-celled dinoflagellates to jellyfish, salps, starfish

The light emitted from the light organ situated below each eye of flashlight fish can be seen up to 100 feet (30 m) away. The Photoblepheron steinitzi *lives in the Indian Ocean.*

and even sharks. Hundreds of applications have been witnessed, and thousands of theories rendered by those tangling with questions such as why some squids have eyes ringed with tiny light spots, while others glow throughout their entire body; why some starfish feature brilliant glowing lines, and others appear to be fully luminescent, and still others have no lights at all.

It appears that light may be used to attract prey to the proximity of a fang-filled maw. Anglerfish are notorious for their exquisitely intricate, illuminated lures, dangled like glistening gems before precisely positioned jaws. The usefulness of a mouth rimmed with bioluminescence — a characteristic of the twelve-foot (4-m), plankton-feeding shark, "megamouth" (*Megachasna pelagios*) — seems fairly obvious. It is easy to imagine small creatures swimming toward what appears to be a shimmering feast, only to find themselves being feasted upon.

Sometimes light is used the way fireflies are known to do, in flashing codes that signal would-be mates. Certain small fish—the "flashlight fish" — are known to shun the light of the sun and moon, but they do respond to flashing messages communicating the whereabouts of the he-fish and she-fish. Light may also startle or confuse a predator, as in the life-saving light show generated by a spectacular little jellyfish called *Colobonema* sp. White lights at the tips of the jelly's tentacles attract predators away from the more vulnerable body or "bell." If attacked, the bell itself may briefly flash a brilliant blue, then turn off coincident with the release of several of the sparkling tentacles — rather like an escaping lizard leaving behind its tail to appease a pursuer. Certain squids and octopuses effect a sleight-of-tentacle escape while confusing predators with a distracting cloud of glow-in-the-dark "ink." A similar strategy is used by various small crustaceans, including shrimp, krill and ostracods.

Among twilight-zone dwellers, hatchetfish employ one of the most remarkable applications of light-for-survival strategies. At first glance, these fierce-looking metallic silver fish seem to be put together all wrong. Large,

*Deep sea fish, such as this marine hatchetfish (*Argyropelecus aculeatus*), use bioluminescence for camouflage and to attract mates and food.*

tubular eyes are directed firmly upward, while a gleaming array of downward-pointing photophores shine blue light along the lower part of the tiny creature's body. A vision comes to mind of someone walking resolutely ahead through a dark forest while pointing a flashlight straight behind. But hatchetfish are very numerous and have a fossil pedigree indicating a long, successful history. Common sense suggests they must be doing something right.

From the standpoint of a creature living where hatchetfish dwell — in a fish-eat-fish world — it would be ideal to be invisible, and "invisible" is the illusion created for creatures approaching hatchetfish from below. The blue belly-lights of the fish are tuned to match the blue light from above, with their intensity varying depending on the ambient light circumstances. Various other mid-water fish equipped with ventral photophores, including the numerous and appropriately named lanternfish, also have the ability to vary light intensity to match changing ambient light. It seems almost certain that the effect of emitting light from below is the obscuring of shadows that would otherwise make the light-bearing creatures visible.

Lanternfish and hatchetfish tend to be black and silver, with a metallic glint that functions as a mirror, providing effective camouflage. In clear water below depths where surface light is significant, or at nighttime, another strategy to achieve the illusion of invisibility is created by fish that have body surfaces with very low reflectivity for blue light. This may explain why many twilight-zone residents are black or dark red, colors that appear dark in the ambient light.

Large masses of creatures living at the edge of light in the sea move up and down, responding to the rhythms of darkness and light. Enormous schools of lanternfish, hatchetfish and certain other fish, as well as numerous kinds of squid, krill, and other small crustaceans, occur in such large quantities that scientists using depth-sounding sonar pick up their echoes and record their images. Long before the true cause of the images was known, many speculated that the source of the repeated shadows on the sonar screen that moved deep by daylight and came close to the surface at night might be biological in nature. Nets towed in the area—referred to as the "deep scattering layer" or simply "DSL"—sometimes brought up shrimp, sometimes squid, sometimes

fish, and always new questions about the nature of that strange, unknown part of the sea.

The one-person sub Deep Rover.

The first direct observations, made in 1966 in the North Atlantic Ocean using the deep-diving submersible *Alvin*, confirmed the presence of huge schools, some five hundred feet (150 m) thick. They were composed largely of lanternfish and hordes of Cyclothone, tiny fish that are believed to be among the most numerous creatures on the planet.

Seven years after using the "Jim" diving system in Hawaii, I began a series of dives in the Exumas using a different kind of diving "suit," one that looks more like an underwater helicopter than a suit as such. Designed by Graham Hawkes, an ingenious British engineer and designer of numerous undersea craft, *Deep Rover* was revolutionary in several respects. Experience gained with various one-man diving systems led Hawkes to focus attention on ease of operation, operator comfort and manipulators with built-in sensory feedback for touch, motion and force. *Deep Rover* looked like a petite, clear, bubble-shaped submarine, with a pair of black, high-tech, crablike arms in front, but it behaved very much like a second skin, a mechanical suit of clothes that could be worn and used almost instinctively. I had piloted the sub on several previous occasions, first during the sea trials in 1984 in Halifax, Nova Scotia, and later for a series of dives in San Diego, California, including two solo descents to the system's maximum rated depth—3,000 feet (900 m).

It was still daylight when my excursion began over the edge of a steep ocean wall along the seaward shore of Lee Stocking Island, one of the outermost of the Bahama Islands. Blue champagne frothed overhead, or so it appeared, as bubbles swirled around the sub and the descent began. David Doubilet and Bob Wicklund accompanied me to nearly two hundred feet (60 m) using scuba tanks. They descended with tight constraints on time and depth; ten minutes required an hour of decompression before they could safely return to the surface. Penguins readily descend to such depths without a scuba tank and stay almost as long. Some seals, such as the Antarctic's Weddell (*Leptonychotes weddelli*), serenely dive as deep as *Deep Rover* and do not even appear especially winded upon returning to the surface nearly an hour later. Sperm whales (*Physeter catodon*) descend deeper still, to more than a mile, remaining submerged for an hour sometimes, readily enduring changes of pressure, temperature and ocean currents that have given many an ocean engineer pause when building undersea craft.

Secure in my one-atmosphere shell, I see Wicklund and Doubilet silhouetted against pellucid blue. One, then another manta ray glides by, and I turn to snap a photo of one of them through *Deep Rover*'s clear hull. Motion along the cliff diverts my attention from the mantas. Squid! Hundreds of them, blue-gray against blue-gray, flying in precise formation, with silver-rimmed eyes turned to inspect this new "creature" in their midst.

At five hundred feet (150 m) the colorful sponges and soft corals characteristic of the near-surface waters have given way to crusts and mounds of other sponge species. Small blades of what appear to be a leafy green algae sprout from crevices in the limestone wall. Some textbooks say plants cannot grow this deep, but the plants have not noticed. Using another clear-sphere

submersible, *Johnson-Sea-Link*, marine botanists Mark and Diane Littler have confirmed the presence of the deepest known plant, a reddish crust prospering at 880 feet (268 m) on a submerged plateau near San Salvador Island, about two hundred miles (320 km) from where I was following the cliff contour downward.

The slope becomes more gradual, and at six hundred feet (180 m) appears shaggy. Remnants of an ancient reef, lightly covered with limey sand and shell fragments, slope downward into the gray-black depths. Using the manipulators, I tug at chunks of coral rock and carefully place them in a container positioned between *Deep Rover*'s "arms." From my seat seven feet (2 m) away, the rock surface appears faintly greenish, sometimes pink, but as barren as moon rock. The apparent lifelessness is an illusion, shattered later when rocks gathered from the ancient reef are examined closely. With a microscope magnifying the view, hidden galaxies of life appear. Three tiny species of brachiopods (lamp shells), several minute patches of encrusting sponges, a glassy crustacean, a translucent segmented worm, a cluster of radically compressed sea lilies—in all, eleven phyla of animals and three divisions of plants on a single chunk of rock. This one small rock hosted a microcosm of life on

Squid, such as the Loligo opalescens, *are remarkable mollusks with a sizeable brain, generally swift movement by jet-propulsion, and the ability to hide themselves by ejecting a blackish liquid or a phospholuminescent material.*

This solitary salp (Thetys vagina) lives in the open ocean.

Earth, written in the lives of microbeasts too small to be apparent from my seat within *Deep Rover*'s glassy shell.

At about 1,000 feet (300 m), a region of deep-sea dunes begins. I head the sub on a course for deeper water, and am confronted with an upward-slanting field of sand forty feet (12 m) high! I stay on course, glide up and over the dune, and continue gradually downward. Other dunes slope to the left, and the right, and another appears dead ahead. As a test at 1,300 feet (400 m), I turn out the lights and wait for my eyes to adapt to the ambient light. I thought I might not see any, but faint images of the pale dunes are apparent, and the sea above appears slightly gray. Straight ahead, there is blackness. The dunes are unexpected. Charts do not show them, and no previous dives have been made in this area beyond 1,000 feet (300 m).

I did expect to see fish and squid and occasional glowing "jellies," and I am not disappointed. At 1,300 feet (400 m), I pause, resting the sub on a sandy slope to check instruments and send a message about my well-being to those waiting on the surface. Lights from *Deep Rover* create an artificial sun in a place where the brightest previous illumination might have been a blue-white flash from a glassy salp or a luminous squid. From the sand, wriggling forms emerge, and soon the sub is sheathed in a living cloud of gracefully moving sea worms, apparently drawn to the sub's dazzling light. I gently disengage *Deep Rover* and move downward.

At 1,500 feet (460 m), a huge rock looms in my path—gray-black, with colorful patches of what appear to be encrusting sponges and bryozoans. From the edge of the rock a large fish—a grouper!—appears, saunters directly over to *Deep Rover*'s dome and peers in. Light this bright must never before have shone into the life of this fish, except, perhaps, during a long-ago larval phase. Certainly no submersible has previously come to call. Is it curiosity that drives this creature to investigate the strange craft that has landed? Two sets of eyes meet. "Who are you?" I want to know. "What is it like to spend your time where day and night subtly merge, where sea worms dance, where the sea is cold and you swim with the weight of forty-six atmospheres pressing down on your scaly hide?" The fish, one known as a misty grouper (*Epinephelus mystacinus*), just stares, moving from one vantage point to another to inspect the sub and its contents. Would I be so serene, I muse, if a spacecraft landed in my backyard? I move the sub slowly toward the rock and the fish follows, but as I move away into deeper water, it remains, perhaps at home among the rock's craggy surfaces.

Traveling deeper, I experience the same sense of wonder I felt as a child, discovering everything new for the first time. Many forms of life are unfamiliar. What is that soft, translucent thing resting on the sand? A sea cucumber? Anemone? A large annelid? A sea cucumber, I think. Yes! Look at that crown of tentacles! A gentle touch with a manipulator causes the small animal to move in a way that confirms its affinity to echinoderms, not anemones or annelids, but what is its name? Have scientists given a name to this deep dweller of the dunes, 2,000 feet (600 m) down, a mile (1.5 km) offshore from Lee Stocking Island in the Bahamas? I do not know. Nor do I know what that glistening, gelatinous being is that is casting iridescent flashes in the sub's bright light. A ctenophore, I decide, as I watch bands of opalescent cilia propel the small creature forward.

Something sparkles in the sand, and I hasten to see what it is. At last, something I recognize, something increasingly common in the deep sea everywhere, something I can immediately name. A beer can, no doubt about it. Idyllic thoughts about the vast, seemingly infinite, wilderness ocean are jarred. "Cans and bottles and bricks and shipwrecks aren't so bad," I remind myself. Each becomes an artificial reef, of sorts—unsightly, perhaps, but not particularly damaging except to the psyches of submersible pilots. Of greater concern is the changing chemistry of the sea, the recent introduction by humankind of huge quantities of substances foreign to the nature of the liquid, living mantle that shapes the character of the planet.

At 2,300 feet (700 m), four hours after leaving the surface, I reluctantly turn an overhead valve to displace *Deep Rover*'s water ballast with stored, compressed air. Slowly, the sub lifts off, and ascends through darkness, sparkling with minute blue-white flashes as the clear dome collides with tens of thousands of small beings. "Like falling into a galaxy," I muse, as I experience sheer delight tinged with worry. Could a change in sea chemistry cause those

lights to dim? If species are lost, who will know? Exploration of the ocean began barely one hundred years ago, and most of it has never been seen, let alone understood. Will we learn enough, soon enough, to care about the fate of small luminous fish, transparent jelly creatures and deep-dwelling dune creatures in the same way that we have come to care about panda bears and cranes and elephants?

I emerge through blue twilight into glittering sunlight. The dive is over, but the real journey has just begun.

This large grouper (Gracila albomarginata) was photographed in the Maldives. When full grown, the largest species of grouper can measure nearly 9 feet (2.7 m) in length and 180 pounds (400 kg) in weight.

THE DYNAMIC ABYSS

PETER A. RONA

THE DEEP OCEAN IS THE LAST FRONTIER ON EARTH AND A SANCtuary for Nature's secrets. Although the abyss has long been regarded as an inaccessible black hole illuminated only by the feeble light of luminescent, lanternlike appendages on bizarre fish, discoveries only now being made are revealing that it is the most dynamic region of this planet. It is the place where the Earth is being created and being destroyed, where exchanges of heat and matter between the Earth's interior and the ocean affect the global environment, where the most spectacular scenery on our planet exists, and where life itself may have originated. Five hundred years after Columbus, the new world lies beneath the ocean.

Our voyage begins in 1964. The British oceanographic research vessel *Discovery* was transiting along the center of the Red Sea from the Mediterranean to join research vessels of other nations in an international expedition to explore the Indian Ocean. A profile of the seafloor 6,900 feet (2,100 m) below was unfolding on a recorder as pulses of sound transmitted from the ship's echo sounder probed the depths. Unexpectedly, a reflective layer appeared about 300 feet (100 m) above the seafloor. How, the scientists wondered, was that possible when solid seafloor is necessary to reflect sound and only water was present?

A year later on another transit through the Red Sea, scientists on board the *Discovery* lowered a temperature sensor and a water sampling bottle at the place where they had observed the reflective layer. The temperature sensor

Opposite:

An anemone (order Actiniaria) adds a dash of color to pillow lava flows. An implement from the Mir *submersible is in the lower right corner.*

recorded hot water near the seafloor where only cold water was supposed to be! Analysis of the water sample revealed that the hot seawater was seven times as salty as normal seawater and greatly enriched in dissolved metals, including copper, iron and zinc. This salty, metal-rich water was dense enough to reflect pulses of sound.

News of the puzzling discovery traveled quickly, and other oceanographic research vessels found similar ponds in seafloor depressions along the center of the Red Sea. A coring device, a pipe thirty-three feet (10 m) long lowered on a cable from a ship, was used to sample the seafloor in some of the ponds. Instead of the usual red clay that covers much of the deep seafloor, the cores recovered brightly colored layers of hot, gelatinous mud, which were phenomenally rich in iron, copper, zinc, silver and some gold.

These chance discoveries in the Red Sea brought to a head a new view of the Earth that had been germinating for many years. The old view was of a static Earth on which ocean basins and continents were permanent features that had existed in their present configuration through much of the planet's history. In this view, the abyss was simply a container for material washed into the oceans from surrounding lands. The revolutionary new view that emerged in the late 1960s was of a dynamic Earth where continents move like rafts as intervening ocean basins open and close and the abyss constantly re-forms.

The puzzling origins of the Red Sea became clearer in this new interpretation of the Earth. Satellite views from space show that the western and eastern coastlines of the Red Sea, now 125 miles (200 km) apart, fit together like pieces of a jigsaw puzzle. Africa and Saudi Arabia rifted apart about ten million years ago. Hot, molten magma still upwells and erupts along the center of the Red Sea, cooling as it rises, then solidifying and spreading to either side of the centerline. These two conveyor belts of new seafloor are rafting Africa to the west and Saudi Arabia to the east at a rate of one inch (2 cm) per year.

At an earlier stage in the opening of the Red Sea, the surrounding land restricted the inflow of seawater from adjacent oceans. Because the seawater evaporated faster than it was replenished in the hot, dry climate, the salt in

A satellite view looking south from the Gulf of Suez down the center of the northern Red Sea. The Red Sea is at an early stage of opening by seafloor spreading, which is rafting Saudi Arabia (left) from Africa (right). The Atlantic Ocean was a narrow sea similar to the Red Sea at an early stage in its opening.

*Female deep sea anglerfish, such as this Johnson's Black Angler-fish (*Melanocetus johnsoni*), attract prey with their dorsal fin ray "lure." Their distensible stomachs allow them to swallow prey that is larger than they are. The males, on the other hand, feed on small organisms. Deep sea anglerfish are found at depths from 1,000 to 13,000 feet (300 to 4,000 m).*

the seawater precipitated onto the seafloor, forming beds more than half a mile (1 km) thick in places. As the Red Sea widened, connections with adjacent oceans opened, the salt precipitation stopped and the salt beds were buried beneath lava flows from volcanic eruptions. Today cold, heavy seawater penetrates down through cracks in the volcanic rocks of the seafloor. During its journey, it becomes saltier as it travels by the buried salt beds and warmer as it flows through hot rocks beneath the center of the Red Sea. In this process, the seawater expands, rises, dissolves metals from the volcanic rocks through which it flows and finally discharges as metal-rich hot springs which pond in low areas of the seafloor. Metallic mineral particles crystallize from the hot springs as they cool, settle to the seafloor and accumulate in red, yellow, white and black layers, reflecting the different metals present.

The Atlantis II Deep, located at the center of the Red Sea next to the original *Discovery* site, some sixty miles (100 km) east of Mecca, contains the largest pond of metal-rich water (six miles/10 km wide) and the richest deposits of metaliferous sediments known in this sea. The bordering coastal states of Saudi Arabia and Sudan have formed a joint commission to determine the feasibility of mining the sediments. When I sailed through the Red Sea in 1979, it was a strange sight to see an American drillship over the Atlantis II Deep. The drillship had been leased by the Saudi-Sudanese Red Sea Commission. It had lowered its drill pipe 1.2 miles (2 km) to the seafloor and was using pumps to suck up the metaliferous sediments. The test demonstrated the feasibility of mining this site and separating out the zinc on the drillship.

Soviet scientists were so intrigued by these developments that in 1980 they attempted to dive to the bottom of the Atlantis II Deep in a three-person research submersible. Their descent was unexpectedly stopped in mid-water near where sound reflections were first recorded. The submersible was too buoyant to penetrate the pond of dense, hot, salty, metal-rich water. Dr. Anatoly Sagalevitch, who piloted the dive, described what he saw when the submersible was stopped at a depth of 6,230 feet (1,900 m), 650 feet (200 m) above the bottom. A distinct boundary was present between overlying clear water and underlying turbid water, which was undulating with the passage of waves like the surface of the sea.

THE WIDENING ABYSS

A pioneering expedition in 1968 that explored the abyss in the eastern North Atlantic off northwest Africa discovered the Atlantic link to the Red Sea. I was Chief Scientist on the research vessel *Josiah Willard Gibbs*, which was cleaving through rough, cold seas and strong easterly trade winds off the southern Sahara desert. The ship towed a sound source that repeatedly discharged blasts of high-pressure air into the ocean. An array of listening devices received the sound reflected from the seafloor three miles (5 km) below and from layers up to a half mile (1 km) beneath the seafloor. We were over the continental rise, an area along the margin of the abyss formed by the accumulation of sediment several miles thick, transported into the ocean from northwest Africa.

A recorder displayed a puzzling profile of the seafloor and the underlying layers. Instead of the usual layers of sediments running parallel to the seafloor beneath the continental rise, the layers formed arches, some of which protruded through the seafloor. Suddenly, an explanation came to mind. The arches might be salt domes. Because salt is lighter than sediment, these bodies of salt push up thousands of yards from salt beds buried beneath layers of sediment. The scientific consensus at that time, however, was that salt beds accumulated only in shallow seas that had undergone episodic evaporation. How could salt beds have been deposited in the abyss? The answer lay in the Red Sea. At an early stage in its opening 180 million years ago, the Atlantic may have been a sea like the Red Sea, where conditions favored the accumulation of thick beds of salt.

This insight was so compelling that I sent a report by radio back to our home laboratory from the ship and arranged a presentation at an upcoming scientific meeting. The idea received some "flak" from colleagues when presented at the meeting some months later. Since then, similar salt domes have been discovered along the eastern and western margins of the abyss of the North Atlantic Ocean and the South Atlantic Ocean, confirming the idea of an Atlantic Sea that was similar to the Red Sea at one time.

Petroleum usually occurs at salt domes. For example, oil and gas production in the Gulf coast region of the United States is generally associated with salt domes. The initial discovery of salt domes beneath the continental rise off northwest Africa has led to an extension of prospects for the occurrence of petroleum in the abyss.

Like the Red Sea, the Atlantic continues to widen. The areas of salt deposits around its margins are the oldest parts of the abyss, which becomes progressively younger and shallower toward the middle of the ocean. Traveling toward the center of the Atlantic, we cross the largest plains on Earth, the abyssal plains at a depth of nearly four miles (6 km). Abyssal plains form where the deepest parts of the seafloor fill with mud and sand transported from the adjacent continents. Rocks eroded from continental mountain ranges gradually break into small particles during the long journey down streams, into rivers, across beaches and through undersea canyons before they reach the floor of the abyss. Fresh leaves have been found buried in sediments of abyssal plains of the equatorial Atlantic, transported to the ocean by tropical rivers like the Amazon.

The abyssal plains are neither perfectly flat nor featureless. Their surfaces are crisscrossed by subtle channels where sediment-laden seawater has flowed down imperceptible slopes, and are marked by hieroglyphic patterns and burrows produced by worms and other small bottom-dwelling creatures. Fields of golf- to tennis-ball-sized nodules are found in the areas of abyssal plains that are most isolated from the input of sediment. The nodules contain variable amounts of manganese, iron, copper and cobalt and are formed over millions of years by the slow precipitation of these metals from the overlying seawater and the underlying sediment.

Continuing the traverse to the middle of the Atlantic, we find that the volcanic rocks of the seafloor emerge from the cover of the abyssal plains and steadily rise nearly 2.5 miles (4 km) over the 1,250 miles (2,000 km) to the crest of the Mid-Atlantic Ridge. The Mid-Atlantic Ridge is a submerged volcanic mountain range that runs along the middle of the North Atlantic Ocean and South Atlantic Ocean and links with other submerged volcanic mountain ranges, which extend beneath all the oceans of the world. A valley — typically about six miles (10 km) wide with walls one mile (2 km) high—

Large snails and crabs move over two mineralized chimneys in a field of hot springs in the Lau Basin of the southwest Pacific. The orange color is the rusting of iron on the chimneys.

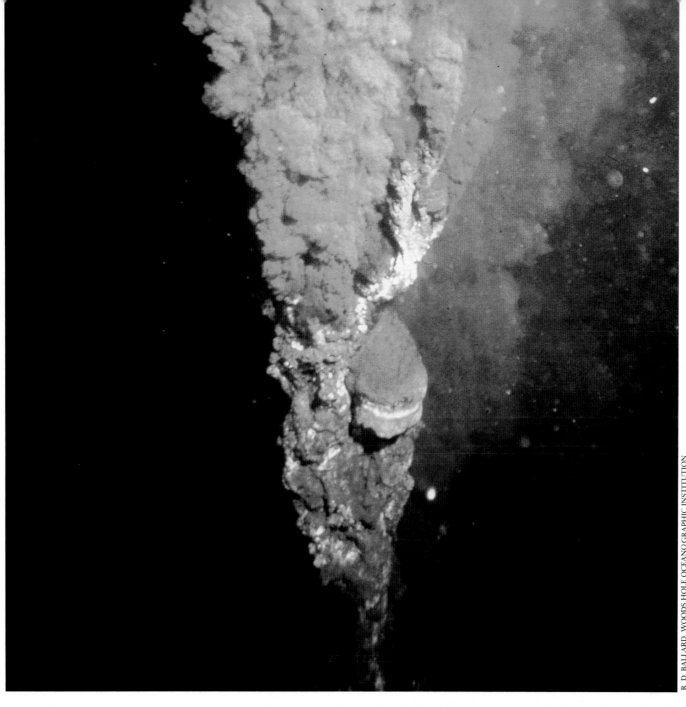

The hottest underwater hot springs, black smoker geysers, discharge water laden with metallic mineral particles from mineralized chimneys on the deep sea floor.

runs along the center of the Mid-Atlantic Ridge and is called the "rift valley." It is time zero in our traverse from the oldest area of the abyss at the Atlantic margins. It is the place where the seafloor is spreading, where volcanic eruptions occur and where we are making our most spectacular discoveries.

After metal-rich hot springs were first found in the abyss at the center of the Red Sea in 1965, the next question was whether such hot springs would occur at submerged volcanic mountain ranges in open oceans. The consensus of the scientific community at that time was that the hot springs were somehow uniquely related to conditions in the Red Sea. On the expedition I led to the Mid-Atlantic Ridge on the U.S. National Oceanic and Atmospheric Administration (NOAA) ship *Discoverer* in 1972, we lowered a chain bag on a cable two miles (4 km) down to the seafloor in the rift valley in the standard technique of dredging to sample rocks. This technique, which is used to this day, is like trying to sample rocks on the surface of the land by lowering a bucket on a rope down through thick clouds from a hot-air balloon. Among the volcanic rocks recovered in our dredge was an unusual black slab two inches (5 cm) thick. The slab was analyzed as almost pure manganese and could only have been deposited from warm springs on the seafloor.

Ignoring skepticism in the scientific community, I launched expeditions in successive years in pursuit of small clues that would indicate the presence not only of warm springs, but of very hot springs. I was encouraged by the occurrence of hot springs in Iceland, which is part of the oceanic ridge that emerges in the North Atlantic. The hot springs are so abundant there that they are used to heat homes and generate electricity. In fact, the word "geyser" originates from a placename in Iceland where hot springs spout from the ground. It is quite a different challenge to locate the sources of hot springs in the ocean by lowering instruments on long cables from a ship in terrain as mountainous as the Alps.

Discovery came all at once on an expedition that I led in 1985 on the NOAA ship *Researcher*. For the first time, our towed cameras imaged black smoker geysers in the Atlantic, and our dredge recovered specimens of poly-metallic sulfide minerals deposited by the hot springs and a new variety of shrimp with unique adaptations. The discovery generated such excitement in the scientific community that the usual two-year waiting period for the research submersible *Alvin* was circumvented. Less than a year later, I entered this new world two miles (4 km) deep in the rift valley of the Mid-Atlantic Ridge and viewed it directly through *Alvin*'s portholes.

The floodlights of the submersible barely illuminated ten yards (9 m) ahead. We gradually made out a mound the size and shape of the Houston Astrodome sports stadium. The hot springs had formed this deposit of metallic minerals, which were colored brilliant red, yellow and orange at the mound surface. The hottest hot springs, black smoker geysers at temperatures of

A white bacterial mat grows on the volcanic rocks in a thermal vent community near the Kamchatka Peninsula.

690°F (365°C), discharged billowing black clouds of metallic mineral particles through steeple-shaped mineralized chimneys up to tens of yards high at the top of the mound. Gray shrimp about two inches (5 cm) long with a curious reflective patch on their backs swarmed over the active black smoker chimneys like bees on a hive. We named this new variety of shrimp *Rimicaris exoculata* (dweller in the deep without eyes) because they lacked eye stalks. Studies of the specimens we brought back with us by biologists at Woods Hole Ocean-ographic Institution revealed that the shrimp were feeding on bacteria that grow in the hot springs. The reflective patch on the back is a novel type of eye that enables the shrimp to sense infrared radiation from the hot springs. Moving outward from the top of the mound, we encountered dome-shaped chimneys yards high venting blue-white smoke at temperatures of 570°F (300°C). Clear, warm water that shimmered in the submersible's floodlights seeped from the mound.

In sediments near the active mound, we found a field of mysterious creatures. Each one resembled a small Chinese checkers playing board the size of a poker chip with rows of tiny holes arranged in a symmetrical hexagonal pattern. A paleontologist who studies the record of ancient life has identified our photographs of these forms as a living fossil, a creature previously known only as it was preserved in ancient marine sediments tens to hundreds of millions of years old.

The discoveries continue. On a 1991 dive series to this site with Russian colleagues and their two state-of-the-art *Mir* ("Peace" in Russian) submersibles, we found a huge mound half a mile (1 km) in diameter. The mound, no longer active, is topped by mineralized chimneys up to twenty-five yards (23 m) high. The active and inactive mounds at this site are similar to many ancient polymetallic sulfide mineral deposits that were formed under similar conditions on the seafloor in the geological past and subsequently uplifted onto land. Many of these ancient mounds on land are mined as important sources of copper, zinc, silver and gold. The Noranda deposits in eastern Canada, which formed on the seafloor 2.6 billion years ago, are an example of this phenomenon, indicating that seafloor hot springs have been present for at least half the 5 billion years the Earth has existed.

THE NARROWING ABYSS

The Pacific abyss encompasses submerged volcanic mountain ranges and abyssal plains similar to those in the Atlantic with one major difference. The Pacific is gradually narrowing by destruction of seafloor to compensate for the widening of the Atlantic by creation of seafloor at the Mid-Atlantic Ridge. Around most of the Pacific perimeter the seafloor bends down into trenches, descending at rates of several inches per year, and melts in the Earth's hot interior. These trenches are the deepest places on our planet. The deepest site known is the Challenger Deep at 6.8 miles (10.9 km) in the Mariana Trench near the island of Guam. In 1960 the U.S. Navy submersible *Trieste* carrying two persons descended for three and a half hours into the abyss, spent twenty minutes on the bottom of the Challenger Deep, where they observed a foot-long flounderlike fish lying on the sandy seafloor, and ascended for three and a half hours. The dive established in the course of a working day (after years of preparation) the complementary world record to the ascent of Mount Everest. The *Trieste* has since been retired and our capability to descend to the greatest depths no longer exists.

Earthquakes and tidal waves are generated as the seafloor bends and descends into the trenches. Volcanoes erupt from the rocks that melt beneath the trenches to form the "ring of fire" around the Pacific. Where the seafloor descends beneath a trench at a high angle, the volcanoes may form chains of

*A newly discovered variety of shrimp (*Rimicaris exoculata*) and fish inhabit a hot spring 12,300 feet (3,750 m) deep in the Atlantic Ocean.*

offshore islands like Japan, the Philippines and parts of Indonesia in the western Pacific. Where the seafloor descends beneath a trench at a low angle, volcanoes erupt on the adjacent land, which is how the Andes Mountains formed along the western edge of South America.

The cutting edge of exploration in the deep ocean is in the marginal seas between the volcanic island chains and adjacent lands in the western Pacific. The marginal seas are small ocean basins hundreds instead of thousands of miles wide. Many of the marginal seas contain active submerged volcanic mountain ranges similar to those in the oceans. International expeditions with Japanese, French, German and Russian research ships and submersibles are finding wonders in the abyss of these marginal seas: the Jade Field of hot springs in the Izena Cauldron, the crater of an active submerged volcano in the Okinawa Trough of the East China Sea, where new varieties of shrimp, fish and crabs live at a huge mineral deposit that is forming on the seafloor; the White Lady Field in the North Fiji Basin, where a lone, pure-white mineralized chimney discharges transparent, shimmering hot water through old, red-colored mineral deposits littered with dead mussels; the adjacent Lau Basin between the Fiji and Tonga islands, where hot springs are populated by a myriad of red and black snails the size of golf balls. And the discoveries have only begun.

Large areas of the abyssal plains of the Pacific are covered by vast fields of manganese nodules. By the 1950s enough nodules had been collected by dredging from oceanographic research vessels to map many of the fields. The metal content of these nodules varies in different parts of the Pacific. Those with the highest content of nickel, cobalt and copper extend southeast of Hawaii to Central America and are so closely spaced in places that they resemble a cobblestone pavement. Calculations by entrepreneurs of the amount of metals in the nodules and their market value were astronomical. In their calculations, however, they neglected or underestimated the costs of recovering the nodules from the seafloor and refining them. They also failed to consider the availability of the metals from more accessible sources on land and legal questions concerning ownership in international waters. Nevertheless, their high estimates triggered a gold-rush mentality. The underdeveloped nations thought that they were going to be deprived of a potential resource, ripe for picking, by the developed nations.

The United Nations took up the cause as part of the Law of the Sea conferences. It proposed the principle of the "common heritage of mankind" as a basis for developing a legal regime and international authority to recover the nodules in the abyss beyond the jurisdiction of coastal states. The United Nations Convention on the Law of the Sea in 1982 defined provisions for mining the nodules and was adopted by 159 countries. Now it is realized that for legal, technical and economic reasons, commercial recovery of manganese nodules is unlikely until well into the twenty-first century.

The submerged volcanic mountain ranges of the Pacific are awesome not so much for their size—most of them lack the great height and deep central valley of the Mid-Atlantic Ridge—but for their newness. The Pacific seafloor is spreading at rates up to ten times as fast as the Atlantic, so volcanic activity is more abundant and frequent than in the Atlantic. A recent deep-diving expedition at the East Pacific Rise, a submerged volcanic mountain range that extends south from the Gulf of California in the eastern Pacific, reported seeing a community of tubeworms that live at hot springs literally "barbecued" by a lava flow that must have occurred just days before their observation.

My experience of the Pacific abyss is vivid from a recent dive series with the U.S. Navy submersible *Turtle* to other hot springs on the East Pacific Rise. The submersible descended 8,530 feet (2,600 m) in one and a half hours carrying a pilot, copilot and me from the broad swells of the sea surface to a volcanic wilderness on the seafloor. As we slowly glided a yard above the seafloor, the glassy surfaces of fresh lava flows glared like ice in our floodlights. Lakes of lava with flow surfaces frozen in fantastic swirls filled depressions hundreds of feet wide. In some places, the bottom suddenly disappeared beneath us leaving the submersible suspended in black space. Solitary columns of rock unexpectedly loomed in the darkness. They were remnants of lava lakes that had collapsed when molten lava drained from beneath the lake surfaces. Vertical rock walls would also suddenly materialize ahead of us where crustal movements had broken and displaced the lava flows.

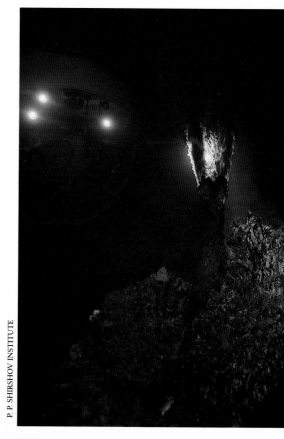

P. P. SHIRSHOV INSTITUTE

A hot spring venting from the top of a mineralized chimney catches the light from a Mir *submersible.*

*Vent worms (*Riftia pachyptila*) about 3 feet (1 m) high grow from a crack between pillow lava flows on the deep seafloor.*

As we approached the hot springs, white flocs of bacteria drifted by like snowflakes and bacterial mats appeared like patches of white paint on the rocks. The hilly seafloor became flatter in the area of a pillow flow, a lava flow with pillowlike forms on its surface. Warm water seeping out through cracks between the pillows shimmered in our floodlights. Giant clams, each half a yard (.5 m) long, stood on edge in the cracks feeding on the bacteria that grow in the warm water. Tubeworms up to two yards (2 m) long stood in clusters with one end of their white tubes attached to the seafloor and bright red plumes, which function as breathing organs, protruding from the other end. White crabs scuttled over the seafloor and climbed on the tube-worms. Gliding into the darkness around the field, we encountered what appeared to be the trunks of giant trees up to twenty yards (18 m) tall — mineral chimneys blasting hot black smoke from vents at the top.

This place is called Clam Acres by biologists, a special site where they come to study the ecosystem of the hot springs. It astonished them that the animals in Pacific vent communities differed so completely from those in Atlantic vent communities and that communities differed even within the same ocean. The differences in vent communities pose unanswered questions about the migration and evolution of vent animals. The single feature common to the abyssal vent communities of the Atlantic and Pacific is the role of bacteria at the base of the food chain. These bacteria use hydrogen sulfide and certain other dissolved gases transported by the hot springs from the underlying rocks as a source of chemical energy to convert carbon dioxide in seawater to carbohydrates for nourishment. These chemosynthetic bacteria are thus dependent on the internal energy of the Earth and independent of the light energy of the sun, which drives the process of photosynthesis in plants at the base of the food chain on land. Biologists are finding archaebacteria, ancient strains of bacteria, at the hot springs. Speculation is growing that life itself may have originated by chemosynthetic processes at hot springs in the ocean rather than by photosynthetic processes on land.

THE GLOBAL ABYSS

When the *Apollo* spacecraft circled the moon on missions in the 1960s it was said that we knew more about the backside of the moon than we knew about the bottom of the ocean. Since then, we have obtained our most complete picture of the inner space of our planet from outer space. The *Seasat* satellite that orbited 620 miles (1,000 km) above the Earth for three months in 1978 used radar to make precise measurements of the height of the sea surface. Analysis of the data revealed that the gravitational attraction of the mountains, valleys and plains of the abyss created corresponding variations in the height of the sea surface so that the sea surface mirrors the deep seafloor on a reduced scale of inches to feet. Maps based on these data show the shapes of the submerged volcanic mountain ranges extending beneath all the oceans, the deep trenches around the Pacific, the vast abyssal plains, and the margins of the continents around the abyss. Of course, this technique does not work for ice-covered areas in the Arctic and around Antarctica. The big picture of the abyssal seafloor sketched remotely by satellite is helping to guide the exploration by surface ships and submersibles, which has only covered a tiny fraction of the abyss as yet.

Discoveries being made are changing our view of the abyss from a passive receptacle to a dynamic system where exchanges of energy and matter between the Earth's interior and the ocean affect the entire planet. These changes are driven by the creation and destruction of seafloor. The circulation of seawater through the hot rocks of submerged volcanic mountains is a two-way chemical exchange process that removes certain constituents from seawater and adds other constituents from the Earth's interior to keep the composition of the oceans hospitable for life. The hot springs are part of an ecosystem dependent on the internal energy of the Earth. This ecosystem is a preserve of biodiversity, a sanctuary for ancient forms of life, and a place where life may have originated.

The new world of the abyss is a place of great wonder and awe. A misguided vision of it as a treasure trove of instant mineral wealth motivated many nations to come together in an international treaty on the oceans. The awareness of the oceans and the relations between nations established by that effort provide a basis for international collaboration to conserve the abyss. We now realize that processes in this part of the ocean impact upon the Earth's entire environment. We must advance our understanding of the abyss and insure its integrity as a dynamic region that plays a major role in the balanced working of our planet.

A jellyfish glows brilliant red in the lights of a Mir *submersible.*

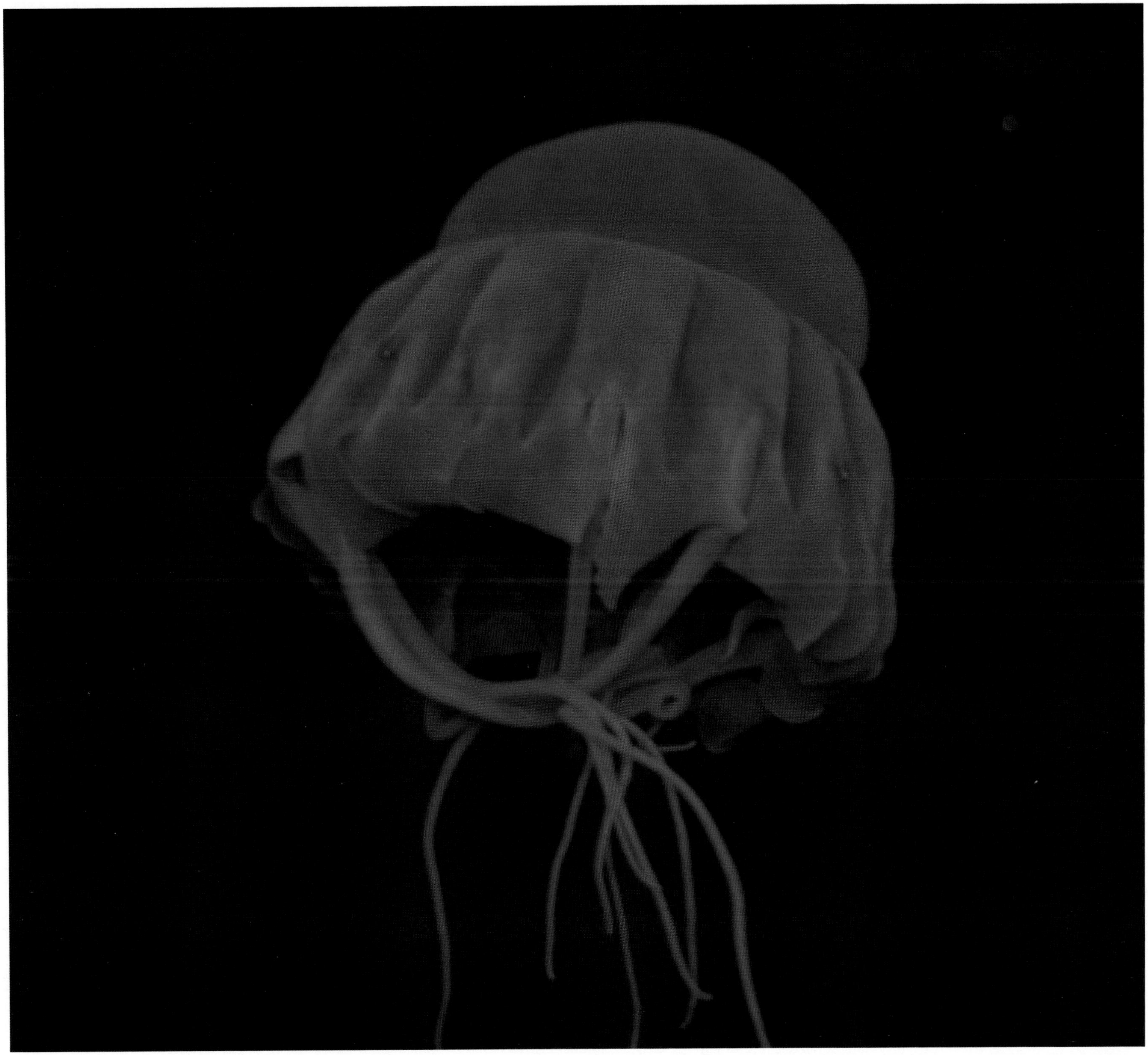

P.P. SHIRSHOV INSTITUTE

ANIMALS AND BIRDS OF THE SEA

Opposite:

The small population (under 4,000) of the Australian sea lion (Neophoca cinerea) *is protected by law.*

The air-breathing animals and birds that live in and by the ocean are not as diverse as the life forms that inhabit its depths. A number of them are protected by law, but all are in need of protection from man-made threats to their environment. These threats include overhunting, habitat destruction or degradation, contamination by toxic materials, and depletion of an animal or bird's food supply.

Above:

Royal albatrosses (Diomedea epomophora) *live on the open ocean, returning to land only to nest.*

During the breeding season, walrus (Odobenus rosmarus) *congregate in herds. They feed together and haul out on the Arctic ice to rest. In the past, they have been ruthlessly hunted for their ivory tusks.*

In the nineteenth century, the southern elephant seal (Mirounga leonina), *the largest and heaviest seal in existence, was hunted to the brink of extinction. Hunting of this seal has been banned since 1964.*

*The polar bear (*Thalarctos maritimus*) is the largest living carnivore on Earth. It depends on the Arctic seas for its primary food source, seals. Hunting of this magnificent animal is regulated by the International Agreement on Conservation of Polar Bears.*

FRED BRUEMMER

*A South African fur seal (*Arctocephalus pusillus*) rookery on the west coast of Namibia. Seals congregate to give birth, making them very vulnerable to predators, including human hunters. At one time the population of this species had been greatly reduced by hunting, but the hunt is now regulated and the population numbers approximately 850,000.*

FRED BRUEMMER

JEFF FOOTT

A blue-footed booby (Sula nebouxii) *preens its chick. These unusual-looking seabirds breed in colonies, usually on islands.*

JEFF FOOTT

The American black oyster-catcher (Haematopus bach-mani) *is uniquely adapted to live along the northeastern Pacific coast. It uses its flattened beak to pry open the shells of limpets and other mollusks and to dig in the sand for crabs and worms.*

JEFF FOOTT

Left:
The black-legged kittiwake (Rissa tridactyla) *is the only true gull of the open ocean. It rarely returns to land except during the breeding season, when it makes its nest of water plants and mud on rocky cliffs.*

Opposite:
Although beluga whales (Delphinapterus leucas) *are still generally abundant, some local populations of these arctic mammals are severely threatened.*

THE SENSORY WORLD OF THE DEEP

JOHN LYTHGOE

I T DID NOT SEEM VERY IMPORTANT AT THE TIME, BUT A BRIEF SWIM WITH a face mask off a Singapore beach was to shape my future career. I was just nineteen years old, serving out my draft in the British Army and without a clear idea of what I wanted to do with my life after completing university. Because the water was thick with sand, it was difficult to see very far. The surge also made it impossible to stay in one place. Suddenly out of the murk appeared a flotilla of tiny, iridescent blue-and-yellow fish, which were swept away by a wave only to be replaced by a dozen equally tiny black-and-white fish. In an effort to stay still, I grabbed what looked like a sea fern and was immediately rewarded by a burning pain and a nettle rash that lasted for weeks. Despite this painful encounter, the overall experience planted a friendly mental virus, which years later led me to begin my life's career studying the vision of fish.

I never had any regrets, because fish have one of the most beautifully adapted visual systems of any group of animals. Color is at least as important to them as it is to us. With all their finely tuned vision, however, fish cannot see further than fifty yards (46 m) or so, and often they can only see a few feet or inches. Aquatic animals have developed other senses that take the place of vision. Some, such as taste, smell and hearing, are familiar to us. Others, such as their electrical sense and the ability to sense movement from a distance, are completely outside our own experience. Over hundreds of millions of years, evolution has perfected sensations and communications in the underwater world that we are only beginning to understand. The ocean is a library of knowledge and we cannot afford to lose one page of it.

Opposite:
Although a worldwide ban on hunting humpback whales (Megaptera novaeangliae) *has been in force since 1966, their recovery has been slow; the current population is estimated at 9,000.*

123

OCEAN COLORS

The radiant dark blue of the light in the ocean is difficult to describe. Although a glass of water may look clear and colorless, at a depth of ten feet (3 m), the natural blue color of water begins to appear. About one hundred feet (30 m) under the surface in the open ocean, the visual scene is dominated by an ultramarine blueness. As you sink farther down, the blue deepens until at a depth of five or six hundred feet (150 to 180 m), the light becomes too dim for color vision and everything is seen in monochrome.

Underwater swimmers will quite rightly object that in their experience the water is more often green, yellow-green or even brown. Furthermore, it is common to run out of light at a depth of one hundred feet (30 m) and sometimes even less. For example, the waters of Chesapeake Bay on the eastern seaboard of the United States, the English Channel and the kelp forests off California vary from blue-green to green. At the extreme end of the scale, some inland waters are brown or even red-brown. The green in greenish water is derived for the most part from the chlorophyll in tiny planktonic plants, while yellow and brown colors can be traced to the tea-colored tanninlike compounds produced by rotting vegetation.

The color of the water affects the appearance of animals and plants underwater. Because red is filtered out in daylight, red fish and corals tend to look black at depths greater than about fifty feet (15 m). This serves to camouflage them. Yellows and blues continue to be visible at depths where it is too dark to see other colors. White is almost always conspicuous, especially if there is a pattern of white on a black background.

Plant plankton grow well in water that is rich in nutrients, and their chlorophyll is an important coloring material in coastal water. Chlorophyll absorbs both blue and red light, leaving the green rays to penetrate deepest. In these waters, it is the orange, red and peacock-blue colors that show up best, although white is also very visible. The level of nutrients in the water can be significantly increased by agricultural chemical runoff or sewage dumping and can be responsible for changing blue water to green. In turn, this reduces the depth that marine plants can grow and fish can see, as well as

AL GIDDINGS/OCEAN IMAGES, INC.

The great white shark (Carcharodon carcharias) uses a number of sensory devices to navigate and find its prey. Because it roams the world ocean, it is difficult to gauge whether its numbers are increasing or decreasing, but concern is growing that it may be threatened by trophy hunting, trade in its jaws and other parts as souvenirs, and commercial fishing.

changing the appearance of some colors. Perhaps these are important effects, perhaps they are not; at present we simply do not know.

Over the past ten years, we have begun to realize that the color of the water has an enormous influence on the color vision of fish. The breakthrough came when instruments were developed to measure the light-sensitive pigments responsible for color vision in the human eye. The same techniques have been used to study the color-vision pigments in fish living in different types of water. We tend to assume that our color vision is rather excellent — and it is compared to many other mammals. Compared to fish, however, it is marginal at best. The humble goldfish can see ultraviolet and infrared light. The reason for the infrared vision is probably to take advantage of the fact that in lakes and rivers where the water is heavily stained brown with tannins, blue and green light is absorbed, leaving mostly red and infrared light to see by. Ultraviolet vision appears to be present only in shallow-living fish and may have something to do with the visualization of the tiny floating animals on which they feed.

Following pages:
Garden eels (Gorgasia sp.) build colonies of burrows in the sand near coral reefs. They feed on plankton, which they find in the water as they sway back and forth. © DAVID DOUBILET

The cells in the retina of the eye responsible for color vision are called cones. Humans have three types, one most sensitive to blue, one to green, and one to yellow-green. Only the yellow-green cone is sensitive to red light and is generally referred to as the red cone. Fish living in deep rather than shallow green coastal water tend to have two types of cones, blue and green. In these waters, there is little red light and red cones have not been found. Recent work on the fish from the bluest water of the Australian Great Barrier Reef show blue and blue-green cones are present, but not green, and certainly not red cones. At the other extreme, it is likely that fish living in brown freshwater where the light is biased to red have yellow-green and red cones and few blue ones. On the basis of color vision alone, we humans would be most at home in the shallow blue-green waters surrounding much of the world's coastline.

Many fish migrate long distances to their breeding grounds or to find other sources of food. In doing so, they may have to travel from green to blue water and back again. Some fish actually seem to change their visual pigments for the journey. Salmon and trout, for instance, have vision that is typical of freshwater fish when they are in rivers and lakes and then develop vision typical of coastal fish when they move out into the sea. American and European freshwater eels also undertake extraordinary journeys in the course of their lives. Although the American eel (*Anguilla rostrata*) and the European eel (*A. anguilla*) are different species, they both begin and end their life cycles in the deep blue waters of the Sargasso Sea in the western Atlantic. Most of their lives, however, are spent in the muddy rivers, ponds and ditches of North America and Europe. During their life span, they change their body form three times from zooplankton, to familiar eel, to deep-sea fish.

The tiny eel hatchlings are so different from the adult eel that they were once thought to be a completely different species. The larvae are shaped like an elongate leaf and are quite transparent. Many other members of the zooplankton adopt the same trick, and it is only after several minutes of staring into apparently empty water that the diver finds that it is full of small jellyfish, mollusks and other forms of life. The leaf-eel is a predator and must catch these diminutive animals to stay alive.

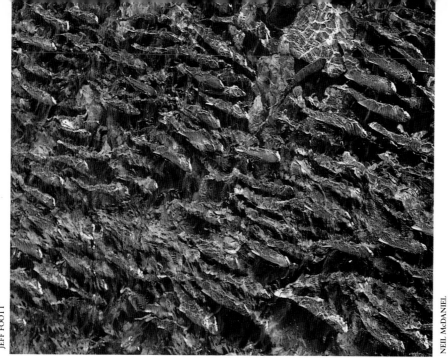

JEFF FOOTT

NEIL McDANIEL

Spawned in slightly different areas of the Sargasso Sea, the North American and European eels are taken by the prevailing currents to their separate destinations. By the time they reach outer coastal waters, the leaf-eel of both species is between two and three inches (5 to 7.5 cm) long. Here a profound body change takes place; their shape becomes rounded and recognizably eel-like. At certain times of the year, which differ from place to place, enormous numbers of the young eels swim inshore and up rivers. They are still transparent in the earliest stages of this journey, and their vision seems to be in an intermediate stage between that typical of green coastal water fish and that of fish living in yellow-green or brown freshwater. Within days, they begin to develop tiny brown spots on their bodies, and within a week or two they wear the olive-brown livery with its iridescent golden sheen that they keep for their entire stay in freshwater and that gives them the name "yellow eel."

Yellow eels spend most of their days buried in mud or wedged into crevices. At night they emerge to feed on almost any kind of animal, living or dead. Freshwater can be exceedingly murky, so vision is not always a useful sense to have. Instead, eels have a greatly developed sense of smell; only a few molecules from a potential food source need enter their nostrils for them to sense it.

After several years, the eels reach adult size — American female eels are about three feet (90 cm) in length, the males, two feet (60 cm), and the Europeans, generally smaller — and the urge to breed takes over. Again, the eels undergo dramatic bodily changes to prepare them for the long ocean

Spawning sockeye salmon (Oncorhynchus nerka), British Columbia, Canada. Salmon migrate long distances to their breeding grounds. Their vision is typical of freshwater fish when they are in their home rivers, but of coastal fish when they move out to sea. Overfishing and pollution of spawning rivers threaten all Pacific salmon.

The killer whale (Orcinus orca), *like all members of the dolphin family, relies on underwater sound for communication and echolocation.*

journey that is to come. To help camouflage themselves from ocean predators, their body sheen changes from golden yellow to silvery, and the ground color from olive or brown to black on the back and whitish silver on the belly. For some reason, scales become more evident and the body becomes less eel-like and more rigid. Their eyes, which were not very useful in their freshwater habitat, now begin to enlarge to give them the more sensitive vision they will need in the deep sea. Sensitivity to color also changes, becoming more like that of deep-sea fish. The apparatus for sensing water currents becomes more developed, while the nose, which will no longer be as useful, is reduced in size.

The eel's new body form suits it for life as a deep-sea fish. The simple fact that these eels are never caught leads one to wonder what else may be down there, unknown to science. For example, although we know that giant squids sixty feet (18 m) long inhabit the ocean, they are unknown as living animals. We know of them only because they are occasionally found washed up on the shore around Newfoundland and their indigestible beaks are found in the stomachs of sperm whales.

HEARING UNDERWATER

It is natural to emphasize the sense of sight underwater, because when we use a face mask, our vision works as well underwater as on land. Our sense of hearing also works quite well underwater, but we are unable to speak properly with our heads submerged. Communication is thus more difficult for us underwater than it is for other animals.

On land, sound waves come through our outer and middle ear and are transformed by the eardrum so that they can be picked up by nerve endings in the inner ear and transmitted to the brain. Underwater, the eardrum does not function and sound is conducted to the inner ear through the bones of the head, just as it is in whales and dolphins. Our ability to hear differences in pitch is scarcely impaired; in fact, synchronized swimmers say they can often hear the music more clearly underwater than on the surface, where it sometimes echoes in cavernous rooms.

Sound travels five times faster underwater than through the air, and it also travels farther. Under very favorable conditions, sounds have been known to travel up to ten thousand miles (16,000 km) through the ocean. It is not outside the bounds of possibility that one deep-diving whale could communicate with every other deep whale in every ocean of the world. However, the propagation of sound through water is a rather chancy business and can be distorted or curtailed by nearness to the surface, layers of differing salinity or temperature, and the nature of the seabed.

The great distances that sounds can travel underwater make the underwater world very noisy. Divers can hear the sound of surf, rain falling on the water, fish grazing the algae from rocks, and the sharp pistol-like noise of snapping shrimps. As is often the case, it is not inadequate sensitivity that

Humpback whales (Megaptera novaeangliae) *gather at a feeding ground off Alaska, USA.*

limits what can be heard but unwanted noise. A new and unwelcome source of noise for fish, particularly shallow-water fish, is the noise made by boat engines. This noise is produced at the sound frequencies to which the majority of fish are most sensitive. Nobody knows if this is a real problem for fish attempting to communicate with one another, but at least one scientist has remarked that there is an evolutionary pressure on fish to shift their most sensitive hearing to receive higher or lower pitched sounds so that they can communicate more easily above or below the sound of boat engines.

On land, we can usually see things at a greater distance than we can hear them. Underwater, the reverse is true. In the clearest water, two whales swimming at the same depth are liable to lose sight of each other at about one hundred feet (30 m), but can keep in touch by sound at a virtually unlimited distance. It is thus not surprising that sound plays such an important role in the lives of whales and dolphins.

The humpback whale (*Megaptera novaeangliae*) spends the summer feeding in polar waters and in the winter migrates over thousands of miles to more tropical locations in the Atlantic and Pacific to breed and give birth. One particular group spends the summer feeding off the Alaskan coast and migrates south to the waters around Hawaii to breed. Although humpbacks are usually silent on their northern feeding grounds, when they reach their breeding grounds, sound becomes very important. Males swim away from the group and "sing" for twenty minutes without repeating themselves. The song is a series of moans, groans, squeaks and clicks—words that give little indication of its ethereal beauty. Each group of whales has its own dialect, and each year the song is different. Perhaps in a world where a whale may by chance hear the song of another thousands of miles away, song dialects are important to prevent a sort of global confusion. However, nobody knows the reason for the songs themselves. Recorded whale songs played back through underwater microphones sometimes, but not always, attract other whales, but there is no evidence that they serve as warnings or serenades. Clearly, such a complex signal must have a purpose; the fact that we do not understand it only goes to show how little we know about the society of these giant creatures.

A southern right whale (Euba-laena glacialis) calf. This slow-moving, trusting giant was easy prey for whalers, who called it the "right" whale because it yielded the longest whalebone and the thickest layer of blubber. Today it numbers only a few thousand worldwide.

Unlike humpback and other baleen whales, toothed whales and dolphins use sound as sonar to "visualize" the world about them. They produce sound by forcing air between a series of air sacs situated between the lungs and the blowhole. The sound is then projected as a focused beam into the water by the oil-filled melon on the forehead of dolphins and the spermaceti organ of whales. Dolphins can hear low notes about as well as humans, but are much

*This electric ray (*Torpedo sinuspersici) *can deliver a powerful electric shock.*

more sensitive to high notes. A young person can hear sounds as high-pitched as 20 kilohertz, whereas a dolphin can certainly hear up to 150 kilohertz and probably up to 200 kilohertz. The higher frequencies are used in their sonar system and are similar to those used by insect-eating bats.

Sonar, whether from bats, dolphins or ships, works by projecting sound into the environment and listening to the echoes that return. By comparing the pitch of the echoes with that of the sound they send out, dolphins can tell whether objects are moving toward or away from them. They can also tell what material objects are made of; for example, the swim bladders of fish make particularly good reflectors, and it may be that the reduced swim bladders in some open-water tunalike fish are intended to hide these fish from hunting dolphins. Unfortunately, there are limits to the dolphin's ability to "see" small objects. A wire less than one millimeter in diameter will be invisible to them, which may be why they are so often caught in the fine mesh nets set to catch tuna. Sound reflectors attached to such nets are said to reduce the accidental killing of dolphins by warning them of the net's presence.

THE UNKNOWN SENSE

We can have some understanding of the underwater world of sights and sounds, because our eyes and ears are not so very different from those of certain marine animals. However, the electrical sense that almost all sharks and rays seem to have is quite alien to us. A distinction must be made between fish that stun their prey by massive electric shocks every bit as strong as from a car battery, and those that produce tiny electrical fields which they use for communication and navigation. There are also many sharks that do not produce electricity themselves, but are supremely sensitive to electrical fields in the environment.

The electric ray has a curious disk-shaped body and a massive electric-producing organ behind each eye. It creeps up on its prey, envelopes it with its wings and stuns it with a massive 200-volt shock. I can testify to its strength, because I once absentmindedly chivied one out of the sand with a bare hand to get a better photograph. The resulting shock literally knocked me backwards; the ray swam off and I never did get my photo. Electric shocks of this magnitude would be far too expensive in energy for the fish to use on a minute-by-minute basis. Those fish that create electrical fields around their bodies use much weaker currents. Electrically sensitive fish are able to monitor the distortions in the electrical fields about them and can tell whether a nearby object is an electrical conductor. This sort of ability could be important in deciding the nature of nearby objects; for example, whether an object is a rock or a stationary fish.

The bizarre-looking batfish (Ogcocephalus *sp.) "walks" across the bottom using its pelvic and pectoral fins.*

All sharks and rays have networks of electrosensory organs scattered over their bodies, particularly on the underside near the mouth. These electrical sensors, each most sensitive in a particular direction, are able to detect tiny electrical fields in the water around them. Some of these electrical fields are set up when a fish exposes the membranes of its mouth and gills as it breathes. Sharks have been observed homing into these electrical currents and catching small flatfish, even when they are under inches of sand.

The electrical sense may also be used for long-distance navigation. When an electrical conductor (the body of a fish) is moved in an electrical field (the magnetic field of the Earth), a current is set up in the conductor and the direction of the current shows the direction of the magnetic field. Sharks have electrical sensors which are capable of detecting these tiny currents and which may well be able to tell the shark where it is heading through the vastness of the oceans.

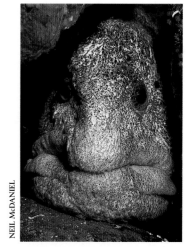

An adult male wolf-eel (Anar-rhichthys ocellatus) *peers out from a rocky crevice.*

In its journeys, the shark carries with it a battery of senses that tell it about a world of which we are only dimly aware. It will be traveling through domains where people have never been, and it will see and sense a world which, for us, remains one of deepest mystery. It is all too easy for us to pollute this world. We have already introduced noise that was not there before. We allow it to be polluted with sewage and fertilizers that alter the color of the water and reduce the depths at which animals can see and algae can reproduce. For all its vastness, this is a fragile world with many secrets. Let us not lose them through greed and neglect.

PROTECTING THE OCEANS

MICHAEL DONOGHUE

THE OCEANS NEED PROTECTION FROM A HUMAN ONSLAUGHT. First, they need protection from the dumping of toxic materials in both sheltered coastal waters and offshore, and from the discharge of sewage sludge into harbors and lagoons. Industrial pollutants accumulating in the oceans become concentrated as they are transferred through the food chain. Near some highly populated areas, fish have become too contaminated for safe consumption and parts of the seabed are almost devoid of life. In other areas of the world, enormous concentrations of deadly pollutants such as polychlorinated biphenyls (PCBs) have been found in the tissues of whales, dolphins and other sea mammals at the top of the food chain. Action is needed to safeguard these and other marine creatures from the toxic wastes of human activities.

Second, the oceans need protection from overexploitation. Fisheries worldwide are declining. The use of destructive fishing methods, such as high-seas drift nets, threatens to affect the ecological balance of entire ecosystems, because many nontargeted fish, mammal and bird species are caught in the nets. Intensive trawling in coastal areas is also damaging the seabed and its inhabitants.

And finally, urgent action is needed to repair the damage that has already been done to the Earth's atmosphere. The thinning of the ozone layer by industrial gases may result in profound changes to the cycle of life in the oceans. In Antarctica, the ozone hole, which recently began appearing each spring, allows the penetration of enough ultraviolet light from the sun to

Opposite:
Like all marine mammals, these hourglass dolphins (Lagenorhynchus cruciger) must come to the surface to breathe. If they become entangled in a net, they will drown.

137

Effluent from the thousands of industrial factories and mills ringing the world ocean, such as this pulp mill on a Canadian west coast fjord, has a cumulative effect on the sea.

threaten the normal patterns of marine photosynthesis. During the spring months, the long hours of daylight allow phytoplankton floating in the surface layers of the Southern Ocean to achieve astonishing productivity. These tiny plants feed the enormous concentrations of krill, the small crustacean at the heart of the Antarctic marine ecosystem. Scientists are now warning that reductions in the productivity of phytoplankton due to increased penetration of ultraviolet light will inevitably disrupt the balance in the rest of the ecosystem.

It is up to all of us to ensure that the oceans are protected from further degradation. We can make our views known in many ways—as individuals, as members of small or large groups, as elected representatives, as informed experts, as ratepayers and perhaps even as activists. This chapter looks at some of the successes other people have had in protecting the oceans, and suggests some ways to help you achieve successes of your own.

HAZARDOUS WASTE DUMPING

"Out of sight, out of mind" has been a familiar attitude toward waste disposal, especially when it comes to dumping all kinds of unwanted material into the ocean. For centuries, the oceans have been the final destination for much of humanity's garbage, but until the twentieth century, the worst effects of this practice were mostly localized. As it becomes increasingly difficult to dispose of wastes on land, however, using the oceans as a dump site has become an attractive option and the consequences have become more widespread.

All over the world, fringes of the ocean are used as furtive dumping areas. The effluent from a large chemical or nuclear factory is much more likely to be the target of public scrutiny than a wood-treatment plant at the edge of a quiet country harbor. Yet the local effects of pollution can be devastating, and the cumulative effects of many sloppy activities around the ocean's shoreline may have profound consequences for all of its inhabitants. This is illustrated by the tragic story of the Canadian beluga.

Although essentially an Arctic species, beluga whales (*Delphinapterus leucas*) have probably lived in the St. Lawrence River since the end of the last Ice Age some 11,000 years ago. While most of the other marine mammals moved northward with the retreating glaciers, herds of these white whales, which had adapted to estuarine living, remained in both the river and the Gulf of St. Lawrence. The high productivity of these cold waters supports beluga year-round and attracts other whale species when the river and gulf are ice-free.

Belugas have always been a traditional food source for indigenous peoples in the Arctic, and since European colonization, they have also been extensively hunted for their hides and oil. The St. Lawrence population was estimated at 5,000 at the beginning of this century, but by the early 1960s had been reduced to about 1,500. Overhunting was the major reason for the decline, although the Canadian Air Force also played a part by encouraging trainee World War II fighter pilots to use the white whales for target practice. Today only 450 to 500 belugas remain. Their habitat, which fifty years ago ranged over 750 miles (1,200 km), from Quebec City to northern Newfoundland,

A ship dumps mining waste at sea off the coast of Australia. Waste from mining and industrial activities can contain heavy metals. These are not broken down in the sea by bacterial action, and they may undergo chemical changes that turn them into even more dangerous compounds.

140   MICHAEL DONOGHUE

is now restricted to a 90-mile (145-km) stretch of the northernmost part of the Gulf, in the Strait of Belle Isle.

The plight of the St. Lawrence beluga was brought to public attention in the 1970s through the efforts of ecologist Leone Pippard, whose extensive research on the white whales provided the proof that decades of overhunting had pushed the population to a perilously low level. After years of intensive lobbying, the Canadian government granted protection status to the St. Lawrence beluga population in 1979.

Yet Pippard's main question remained unanswered—why did the beluga population continue to decline after large-scale hunting had ceased in the 1950s? Analyses of dead whales washed up on beaches during the 1980s have provided the answer. The St. Lawrence River belugas are living toxic waste dumps, because of the accumulation in their bodies of decades of pollution from the industrial cities of the Great Lakes. They contain high levels of a number of organochlorine compounds, in particular PCBs, immensely persistent chemicals that cause sterility and destroy the immune system in mammals. Dead beluga have been found to contain PCBs in excess of 1,750 parts per million (ppm). In Canada, substances containing PCBs in concentrations of more than 50 ppm are deemed to be toxic waste, and must by law be incinerated. In theory this means that well-meaning whale rescuers could be prosecuted for pushing a stranded beluga back into the water! Canadian and U.S. authorities have responded to the public outcry over the belugas' fate by promising a massive cleanup of the St. Lawrence, costing hundreds of millions of dollars. However, even if the cleanup is successfully carried out, it may come too late to save the remaining whales.

Marine turtles, such as this leatherback turtle (Dermochelys coriacea) *in French Guiana, must come ashore to lay their eggs. Populations have declined in tourist areas.*

Another graphic reminder of the desperate need to clean up our oceans has been the recent die-offs of thousands of dolphins. In 1987, hundreds of bottlenose dolphins (*Tursiops truncatus*) washed up on the eastern coast of the United States. In 1989, hundreds more were stranded on the western coast of France. And in 1990, as many as five thousand striped dolphins (*Stenella coeruleoalba*) were found on beaches around the Mediterranean Sea. All of these stranded dolphins had high levels of PCBs in their bodies and depressed or nonfunctioning immune systems.

As consumers, we must insist that all discharges of toxic chemicals into the oceans cease, and, if necessary, we must be prepared to pay more for our goods in order to ensure clean production techniques. Each one of us should remember that pouring weedkiller, waste oil or paint stripper down the drain is also a crime against the environment.

Although a moratorium on commercial whaling has been in effect since 1986, the aftermath of the hunt lingers. Oil stains the beach of an abandoned whaling station.

OCEAN ISLAND WASTE DUMPS

The prospect of rising sea levels as a result of global warming is particularly alarming for island nations in the South Pacific, many of which have a coral base and are only a few yards above sea level. In misguided efforts to boost tourism, engineers in some Pacific island states have used material taken from their own coral reefs to build breakwaters for hotel beach developments. The predictable consequence of such folly is often far greater damage from hurricanes, because the outer reef is no longer able to effectively absorb the power of the waves.

And in a new twist to the old phrase, "Where there's muck, there's brass," several enterprising companies have been trying to entice a number of Pacific islands to stave off the dangers of sea-level rise by accepting domestic waste from the United States for incineration and disposal. Promoters of the idea argue that the governments would not only receive money for allowing the disposal of waste, but would also be able to use the residues after incineration as landfill to raise their islands higher above sea level.

In 1989, mindful of the financial temptations of such deals for poor island nations and the grave environmental risks of filling lagoons with hazardous wastes, members of the European Economic Community and sixty-eight former European colonies in Africa, the Caribbean and the Pacific signed the Lome Convention, banning all toxic and nuclear waste exports. Countries that are not signatories to the convention, however, are still vulnerable to multimillion-dollar deals touted by international waste-traders.

OIL POLLUTION

The transport of oil across the world's oceans presents another grave and persistent threat to marine wildlife. Each year, tens of thousands of tons of oil are routinely discharged into the oceans by tankers during the course of ballasting or cleaning their tanks. Tanker collisions or sinkings also occur regularly throughout the world, most often in the crowded coastal waters that are home to large populations of seabirds and marine mammals.

When oil spillages occur in cold waters, the effects last far longer than in warmer seas, because oil breaks down much more slowly at low temperatures. The impact of the *Exxon Valdez* spillage on the wildlife of Prince William Sound, for example, appears to have been far greater than the impacts on the Persian Gulf of the much larger discharges that took place there during the Gulf War.

The huge fine levied on Exxon as a result of the Alaskan spill should act as an incentive to other companies to ensure that their crews are well trained and their vessels seaworthy; yet no matter how great the financial penalty for the polluter, nothing can alter the fact that it will be decades before the wildlife of Prince William Sound is fully recovered.

Clean-up crews try to remove oil from an Alaskan shoreline after the 1990 Exxon Valdez *oil spill.*

NUCLEAR WEAPONS TESTING

Recognizing the immense power of the atomic bomb, the United States and Britain conducted their postwar nuclear weapons testing programs in the most isolated regions of the South Pacific Ocean. The remoteness of the test areas, in an era that did not have fax machines and satellite communications, ensured that little attention was paid by the international media as islands were destroyed, vast areas of ocean contaminated with fallout and thousands of people displaced from their traditional homes.

In 1963, Britain and the United States signed the Partial Test Ban Treaty in which they agreed to conduct future nuclear tests underground in Nevada. France, however, continues to use the coral atolls of Moruroa and Fangataufa in French Polynesia as sites for testing nuclear weapons. Although the French government assures the world that there are no harmful environmental effects from the tests, independent scientific measurements are not permitted, and warships patrol the twelve-mile (19-km) exclusion zone around the sites.

Little effective protest was ever made against the American and British atmospheric tests in the 1950s and 1960s, but Pacific Island governments, as well as citizens' groups and individuals from around the world, have been vigorously opposing the French testing program for many years. Vessels of all shapes and sizes, including a twenty-four-foot (7-m) trimaran, an old Baltic trader and a square-rigger, have sailed to the test area to bear witness, and in many cases have delayed a testing program. In 1974, when the French government was still testing nuclear bombs in the atmosphere, the New Zealand government took the unprecedented step of sending a frigate to Moruroa with Cabinet Minister Fraser Colman on board. This bold diplomatic gesture helped to drive the program underground, but the testing has continued. The remoteness of the site has undoubtedly helped the French ride out international criticism.

The most vocal critic of the French nuclear testing program in the international media and the most active demonstrator at the test zone has been the international environmental group Greenpeace. The organization's flagship, *Rainbow Warrior*, was sunk in Auckland harbor by limpet mines planted by French commandoes in July 1985. The ship was about to depart for Moruroa, reportedly equipped with sensitive instruments to test for radioactivity. When the mines exploded at midnight, Greenpeace photographer Fernando Pereira was killed and the rest of the crew was fortunate to escape with their lives.

The capture of two of the French agents responsible for the bombing, and their sentencing to a ten-year jail term, provoked a major international incident between France and New Zealand. In retaliation, France placed an embargo on New Zealand agricultural products. Diplomacy prevailed in the end—the agents were deported after only six months in custody, and France withdrew its embargo and paid US$8 million to Greenpeace and the New Zealand government in compensation.

Penguins incubate their eggs for a long time and their young develop slowly. Yellow-eyed penguins (Megadyptes antipodes) live in New Zealand and a few adjacent islands, where they are considered endangered. Here a parent (left) stands with its chick (right).

Despite the troop withdrawals and easing of East-West tensions in Europe, the nuclear weapons testing program in the South Pacific continues. Surely, now is the time for the people and governments of all nations — and in particular French voters — to persuade the French government that there is no further need to destroy coral atolls and contaminate the oceans with radioactivity in the neverending search for better nuclear weapons.

INTERNATIONAL AGREEMENTS

If our oceans are to be effectively protected from the harmful effects of pollution, current international agreements will need to be greatly expanded and new global agreements will need to be developed.

Recognizing the possible dangers in unregulated dumping at sea, a number of international agreements addressing this problem have been negotiated. The most important is the 1976 Convention on the Prevention of Marine Pollution by Dumping of Wastes and Other Matter, otherwise known as the London Dumping Convention (LDC). It specifically covers the deliberate ocean dumping of various industrial wastes.

Article 1 of the LDC requires signatories to the Convention to prevent marine pollution from all sources, and might therefore be expected to prohibit the ocean dumping of radioactive wastes. Until the mid-eighties, however, the United Kingdom and several other European nations routinely disposed of much of their nuclear power industry's wastes into a two-mile (3-km) deep trench in the Atlantic Ocean six hundred miles (1,000 km) west of Cornwall, as they had been doing since the 1960s. The British government claimed that there was no conclusive scientific evidence that the barrels of radioactive waste constituted a source of pollution.

A public campaign was needed to bring the dumping to an end. Greenpeace, which first discovered the dumping area, took the lead by harassing the dump ships in the act of disposing of their cargo. Over a number of years, volunteers in small inflatables attempted to block the disposal of the forty-four-gallon (167-L) drums full of waste, often at great personal risk. The David and Goliath conflict at sea was well publicized in the British media.

CHUCK PLACE

Of the three groups of monk seals, the Caribbean monk seal (Monachus tropicalis) *is now apparently extinct, the Mediterranean monk seal* (Monachus monachus) *numbers only 500, and this one, the Hawaiian monk seal* (Monachus schauinslandi), *numbers only 1,000. Although protected, their numbers are still declining due to human disturbance of their habitat.*

At the same time, Greenpeace was also working closely with the British union movement and had begun a lobbying campaign amongst the membership of the London Dumping Convention. Seven years after the first action taken by the *Rainbow Warrior* against the dump ship *Gem*, members of the LDC voted in 1985 for a moratorium on ocean dumping of radioactive waste. The British government, however, resolved to ignore the LDC ban and announced its intention to continue with the disposal of radioactive waste at sea. Foreseeing this possibility, Greenpeace had already persuaded the

railway unions to refuse to handle any train carrying radioactive waste for ocean dumping. In 1988, ten years after the beginning of the public campaign, the British government, unable to move the waste from its sources of origin, finally agreed to abide by the terms of the LDC resolution.

Despite this success, many other issues still need to be addressed by the LDC. At present, over one hundred nations remain outside the Convention, and there is nothing to prevent a Contracting Party from exporting banned wastes to a nonmember nation, which could then dump them at sea. The Convention also fails to cover the coastal waters of member states. Furthermore, 80 percent of all marine pollution emanates from land-based sources, such as industrial plants, chemical factories, and mining and agricultural activities, which are not covered by the Convention.

In June 1992, the largest environmental conference ever convened will be held in Rio de Janeiro. Among a range of pressing issues, the United Nations Conference on Environment and Development (UNCED), or Earth Summit, will be considering the protection of oceans and seas. Close attention will be given to the problems of pollution, unselective and unsustainable fishing techniques, protection and conservation of endangered marine mammals and other wildlife, and management of the entire marine ecosystem, rather than of just a few commercial fish species. The prominence of the protection of the oceans on the agenda of such an important gathering is a strong signal of changing international attitudes.

REGIONAL AGREEMENTS

In the absence of comprehensive global protection, regional agreements may provide an effective means of protecting the oceans. The Convention for the Protection of the Natural Resources and Natural Environment of the South Pacific (SPREP), for example, commits parties to preventing, reducing and controlling pollution at sea in the South Pacific region. It prohibits the dumping and storage of wastes, including all levels of radioactive waste. The United States, United Kingdom and France have all signed the Convention, which greatly improves the prospects for the waters of the South Pacific to escape the heavy pollution burden carried by seas and oceans in more industrialized areas.

This Hector's dolphin (Cephalorhynchus commersonii) calf has drowned in a gill net. Found solely in New Zealand, the total population of this small dolphin numbers only three to four thousand; many have perished in nets.

The virtues of cooperation between countries to protect the oceans were never better illustrated than in the South Pacific during 1989 when the Tasman Sea and southwest Pacific were invaded by a fleet of almost two hundred Asian driftnet fishing vessels. Each night these ships deployed nets up to thirty-seven miles (60 km) in length. Recognizing the dangers to their own fisheries as well as the devastating effects of driftnets on other species of fish, marine mammals, seabirds and turtles, and spurred on by public opinion, the twenty-two island nations of the South Pacific quickly drafted and signed the Wellington Convention, which closed their two-hundred-mile Exclusive Economic Zones to driftnetters.

At the same time, with the assistance of the United States, whose salmon industry was seriously damaged by the driftnet fleet in the North Pacific Ocean, the South Pacific nations took their case to the United Nations. In December 1989, a landmark resolution was agreed upon which paved the

A mole cowrie (Cypraea talpa) *with its mantle covering the shell and with the mantle withdrawn. Often tourists and buyers of shellcraft are unaware that shells come from living animals and that shell collecting can adversely affect mollusk populations and the ocean habitat itself. Corals may be broken off in search of shells and sandy areas disturbed by trawling.*

J. RANDALL

way for a complete phase-out of large-scale driftnet fishing on the high seas by mid-1992, with a cessation in the South Pacific by mid-1991. Never before had an environmental issue brought before the UN General Assembly had such swift results. Although Japan continued to try to persuade the world that its driftnet fishing could be carried on without environmental risks, it has now bowed to world pressure and agreed to put a halt to this type of fishing by the end of 1992.

NATIONAL AND LOCAL LEGISLATION

As well as international and regional agreements, many countries have national or local laws governing industrial discharges, which in theory should protect our oceans and their inhabitants from chronic poisoning. Too often, however, the laws are ineffective. What is needed is a commitment from all levels of society, business and government to end our use of the ocean as a sink for endless quantities of waste material. More environmentally benign technologies must be developed and used, alongside stricter controls on pollution.

Politicians are finding that an increasing number of voters care deeply about the environment. Outdated environmental legislation is under review in many countries as the importance of sustainable development and providing for the needs of future generations is more widely recognized. As voters, in both general and local elections, we must elect legislators who will ensure that the environment is cleaned up.

WHAT YOU CAN DO AS AN INDIVIDUAL

In addition to lobbying politicians and diplomats, individuals can play a powerful role through their choice of products. Encouraging sustainable and benign technologies in the production of food and manufactured items is best done by supporting them financially. The explosive growth in the sale of "green" consumer products in the last few years demonstrates that many people are anxious to minimize their impact on the planet's resources. One of the most recent initiatives has been the labeling of tuna cans to indicate whether dolphins were likely to have been killed in the fishing process. In Australia and the United States, labeling of tuna cans is now required by law, while in many other countries, supermarket chains and brand leaders advertise that they provide only "dolphin-safe" tuna.

The trend in environmentally conscious consumerism is being noticed by some of the largest multinational corporations. In April 1990, Starkist Seafood, the largest tuna canner in the United States, announced that it would no longer accept tuna that had been caught either by driftnets or by setting purse-seine nets around dolphins to catch schools of tuna swimming beneath. The decision to make a fundamental change in corporate policy after twenty-five years of killing dolphins to minimize the costs of catching tuna was in fact made by Starkist's owner, multinational food giant H. J. Heinz Company. Heinz was worried about the possible costs of a threatened international consumer boycott of their major brand names — most of which are not connected with seafoods.

Boycott campaigns have been very successful in recent years. When Iceland continued to kill whales after the establishment of the moratorium on commercial whaling in 1985, conservation groups in the United States banded together to lead a consumer boycott of Icelandic fish, a trade valued at US$200 million per annum. The fast-food industry was targeted, and several of the largest companies cancelled long-term contracts for Icelandic fish. By February 1989, the boycott was estimated to have cost the Icelandic fishing industry over US$50 million. The boycott was called off only after Iceland announced an end to its "scientific whaling" program in July 1989.

Citizens' groups can also help protect local areas of sea and coastline by promoting the establishment of marine reserves, parks and sanctuaries. Sometimes these areas may be of special scientific interest — breeding places for endangered species of marine mammals or seabirds, for example — but they may also be worth preserving simply for their intrinsic value. Even overexploited areas soon regain healthy populations of fish if a reserve is established

© NORBERT WU 1991

*Strands of an abandoned fishing net are strangling this young California sea lion (*Zalophus californicus*).*

and fishing is prohibited. Marine reserves near urban centers are especially important, giving city-dwellers a rare opportunity to experience wildlife in its natural surroundings.

Faced with continuing pollution of the seas by powerful industries and intransigent governments, individuals and organizations have sometimes chosen to break the law to draw attention to the plight of the sea and its inhabitants. Although the British government was forced to end the dumping of radioactive waste in the Atlantic Ocean, discharges of "low-level" radioactive waste have been permitted to continue from the nuclear fuel reprocessing plant at Sellafield on the northwest coast of England. According to Greenpeace, the Irish Sea, which receives the discharge, is now the most radioactive body of water in the world. In 1983, Greenpeace was fined £50,000 after attempting to block a discharge pipe and refusing to agree not to repeat the action. In 1987, when the *Sirius* returned to Sellafield and successfully blocked the discharge pipe, the vessel's skipper and the action coordinator were both jailed for three months.

Sometimes an individual's actions are able to mobilize an enormous groundswell of public support. For example, Sam LaBudde, an American marine biologist, took his life in his hands in 1988 when he joined a Panamanian tuna boat as a cook and secretly filmed the practice known as "fishing on dolphin." In the Eastern Pacific, yellowfin tuna often swim underneath dolphin schools and are captured by huge purse-seiners, which set their nets around the dolphins in the hope of catching tuna. Over the past twenty-five years, at least 7 million dolphins have needlessly died in this fishery, drowned in the nets or crushed by the power blocks that haul them into the boats. LaBudde was the first person to successfully capture on film this needless slaughter. His horrific images of dying dolphins were widely publicized and sparked the campaign that within two years reversed the corporate policy of all the major American tuna processors.

Around Iki Island, as in other parts of coastal Japan, the local fishermen still fish in a traditional way. They catch yellowtail from small boats, using handlines. Dolphins were often driven into bays and slaughtered on suspicion

*The Sea Turtle Protection Association in Sri Lanka digs up endangered hawksbill turtle (*Eretmochelys imbricata*) eggs and re-buries them in a protected area. Hatchlings are nurtured by staff members and then released into the sea at the appropriate time.*

*A sea otter (*Enhydra lutris*) wraps itself in kelp for the night off the coast of California, USA. Sea otters are threatened by contamination from oil spills and entanglement in gill nets.*

of scaring away the fish. Hawaiian environmentalist Dexter Cate witnessed the killing of hundreds of dolphins from a large herd trapped by fishermen in February 1980 and was appalled at the senseless brutality. He resolved to free the remaining 250 dolphins penned awaiting death, and paddled his kayak through the surf and high winds to cut free the net trapping them. He was later arrested and imprisoned, but his courage and gruesome photographs of the slaughter focused the international media's attention on Iki. Within a few months, he was released from prison and the Iki dolphin kills ended.

Canadian Paul Watson founded Sea Shepherd, an organization that specializes in direct action to protect the oceans. Members are prepared to expose themselves to considerable danger, including jail terms, to make their point. In his best-known action in 1979, Watson sank the pirate whaler *Sierra* by ramming the vessel at dockside.

While the high-profile actions of a few activists can help enormously in focusing public attention on the state of our oceans, most of the concrete protective measures are achieved by the quiet, diligent work of many individuals and groups. In most democracies, the legislative and planning process offers considerable scope for public participation. It was largely due to a worldwide letter-writing campaign that so many countries were added to the membership of the International Whaling Commission during the late 1970s and early 1980s, eventually allowing the conservationist nations to achieve the three-quarters majority needed to establish the current moratorium on commercial whaling. And the battle is still far from won. The whaling nations believe that commercial whaling will be resumed by 1993, and they could well be right unless public opinion keeps the pressure on diplomats and politicians to maintain the moratorium.

Local citizens' or ratepayers' groups can be very successful in protecting their own particular piece of coastline or estuary by lobbying for protected areas and by opposing inappropriate development. As coastal residents or visitors, we can also do our part to protect the seas. Amateur fishers can help by observing catch limits and minimum size limits, and by avoiding the use of nylon gill nets, which can accidentally entangle seabirds and marine mammals. Everyone who spends time on or near the ocean should also be aware of the dangers posed by marine debris. Over 640,000 plastic objects are discarded in the world's oceans each day, according to the U.S. National Academy of Science. Some are extremely hazardous to marine wildlife. For example, seals and sea lions become entangled in scraps of netting thoughtlessly tossed overboard from fishing trawlers, and seabirds often fall victim to the empty plastic rings from six-packs of beer or other beverages. Even the humble plastic bag carelessly tossed from a pleasure boat may be mistaken for a jellyfish by a passing turtle.

Protection of the oceans begins with individuals who care enough about the future to want to make their own contribution, whether it is by carefully selecting the appropriate food or product to buy; by joining and financially supporting one of the many organizations working on protecting the oceans; by working through community groups on specific local issues; by writing letters and articles; or by direct and active involvement. Saving our oceans and their wealth of wildlife, for their own intrinsic value and for the enjoyment of future generations, will only be possible through the concerted efforts of millions of caring people worldwide.

STEPS TO TAKE TO PROTECT THE OCEAN

- Support the establishment of marine reserves, parks and sanctuaries in your country.
- Participate in letter-writing campaigns and boycotts to end practices that damage the sea and its inhabitants.
- Join one of the conservation organizations listed at the end of this book.
- Dispose of toxic materials, such as waste oil, paint stripper and weed killer, in an environmentally safe manner, not down the drain. Better

still, use nontoxic alternatives.
- Retrieve trash found in the water and along the coast and dispose of it properly.
- Participate in local beach cleanups or organize one in your area.
- Encourage marinas and other oceanside facilities to provide adequate trash containers and recycling bins.
- If you own a boat, keep a trash can on board, be sure it is kept covered and make sure everyone on board uses it.

- Place unwanted fishing line in a trash can, not in the water, where it could be harmful to marine life.
- Avoid taking disposable plastic products on board boats, especially plastic bags and six-pack rings. These products are harmful to marine creatures and litter beaches.
- Do not throw cigarette butts overboard. Studies have shown that filters, which do not break down in the sea, are harmful to marine birds.
- Make sure your boat motor is

properly serviced and does not leak gas or oil into the water.
- Never discharge wastes from a toilet onboard a vessel directly into the ocean.
- Use a bilge pillow or sponge in the bilge of your boat to remove oil from water that collects there.
- Use nonphosphate detergents when cleaning your boat.
- Avoid using toxic antifouling paints on your vessel.

EPILOGUE

ANATOLY SAGALEVITCH

Outside the steel hull of my submarine is a cold and lightless world. We are at 4,000 feet (1,200 m), ascending slowly toward our support ship, the *Akademick Keldysh*. I have just piloted my Canadian friend Joe MacInnis and our American colleague Emory Kristof on a fifteen-hour dive into King's Trough between Spain and the Azores. For more than an hour, the three of us were parked on the bottom, suspended between the walls of a colossal canyon, looking out through our thick acrylic viewports. A few yards away was our sister submarine *Mir 2*, and inside, looking across at us, three smiling faces.

For me; our dives into one of the deepest sites in the North Atlantic have been far more than science and exploration. They have been dives of personal discovery. In my thirty years of working under the sea, I never believed that one day a Russian, an American and a Canadian would be sharing the same life-support system 16,000 feet (5,000 m) under the sea.

We live in a world that is changing rapidly and globally. For the past half century, world politics have been hypnotized by nuclear weapons. Now, both in my country and in the West, we are seeking values and actions more attuned to the peacetime challenges of the next century. Our concerns include population growth, the overheating of the planet and the shameful disposal of our toxic wastes. They also include saving the oceans.

Nowhere will this be a greater challenge than in my country. In our rush to industrialize, we have poisoned the White Sea, the Black Sea and the

Opposite:

Marine creatures have developed a number of ways to avoid being eaten by predators. Glands in the fin spines of the lionfish (Pterois) produce a powerful venom.

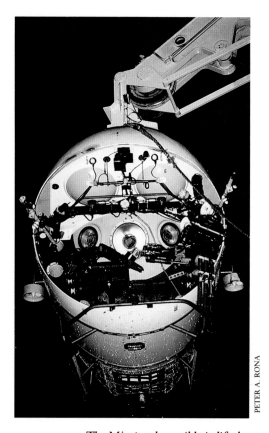

The Mir 1 *submersible is lifted from the ocean by a crane during a nighttime recovery.*

network of rivers and lakes between. But in our beloved Baikal in Siberia, the world's oldest and deepest lake, we reached a turning point. Voices cried out against the loss of a national treasure. The people forced the government to change. Our environmental movement was born.

That incident, which took place almost twenty years ago, convinced me that people working together, sharing a vision, can do anything.

Inside this small seacraft with me are three men who were once rivals. Today, we are partners. We are within arm's-length of each other, sharing each other's thoughts. When you work under the sea with other people, you work hard and carefully because you know their lives depend on you and your life depends on them. Our being here, together, riding the ocean's buoyancy back to the surface and the sunlight, gives me hope.

I have talked at length with Joe and Emory and my other new friends in the West. I know we all want a world where huge sums of money are no longer spent on nuclear arms. We all want a world where our children are no longer forced to give up their youth to war but will join us in a more meaningful struggle—the race to save the ocean.

It will not be easy. It involves a vision of what the ocean should be and a burning commitment to that vision.

The authors and photographers who contributed to this book have given us two things: inspiration and a blueprint. Their inspiration will help us create our own personal vision. Their blueprint, their indication of what is wrong and what we can do about it, will help us design the positive actions each of us can take.

Like peace, the real work of saving the ocean is not only carried out in diplomatic chambers and government offices. It is carried out in the hearts and hands of people. People who think and act. People who care.

Translated from a series of interviews with Joseph MacInnis

ENDANGERED AND THREATENED MARINE ANIMALS

RONALD ORENSTEIN

This appendix provides information on marine animals (including, for completeness, a few species of dolphin found only in freshwater) that have been listed as endangered, threatened or some other comparable category in at least one of three places. The list is primarily based on the *1990 IUCN Red List of Threatened Animals*, published by the World Conservation Union (IUCN), a worldwide association of governments and nongovernmental organizations. Additional species have been included if they receive protection (as of mid-1991) under either the U.S. Endangered Species Act (ESA), which applies to species from around the world, or the Convention on International Trade in Endangered Species (CITES), a 112-member treaty placing restrictions on the import and export of wildlife and wildlife products. I have tried to include all species on these lists that spend at least part of their lives in, or over, the world's oceans. However, I have omitted some land mammals, such as the polar bear,

that visit or even feed at sea. Birds have been included only from families traditionally regarded as seabirds.

Note that these lists are subject to change. The U.S. government has proposed removing the gray whale (*Eschrichtius robustus*) from the ESA. Proposals to be considered at the 1992 CITES meeting in Kyoto, Japan, call for the removal from the Appendices of the northern elephant seal (*Mirounga angustirostris*) and the addition of the queen conch (*Strombus gigas*), herring (*Clupea harengus*) and bluefin tuna (*Thunnus thynnus*).

A list of this type should be used cautiously. Our ignorance of life in the world's oceans is still profound, even after decades of study. The choice of species singled out for inclusion on endangered species lists probably has more to do with that ignorance than with any ability we have, on the basis of current knowledge, to determine which of the sea's creatures are really endangered. Some of the animals listed here may be in no real

danger. More to the point, for every species listed there are probably dozens, perhaps hundreds, of others that are vanishing—without our knowledge—or will vanish if we keep fouling and stripping the seas. Cyanide poisoning on reefs in the Philippines, for example—a technique used to collect specimens for the aquarium trade—has greatly reduced numbers of several reef fishes. Other species may be affected by sudden change. The oil spill produced by the recent war in the Persian Gulf has threatened five coral reef fishes found nowhere else: the Persian dottyback (*Polychromis persicus*, family Pseudochromidae), the mystery butterflyfish (*Aporochaetodon nigropunctatus*, family Chaetodontidae), the arab cardinalfish (*Cheilidopterus caninus*, family Apogonidae), the Persian wrasse (*Halichoeres stigmaticus*, family Labridae) and the arab parrotfish (*Scarus persicus*, family Scaridae).

We do not even know the status of some of the sea's largest creatures. For example, there is a

genus of beaked whales, *Mesoplodon*, found in open seas throughout the world. There are thirteen species of *Mesoplodon*, including one, *M. peruvianus*, described for the first time in 1991. We know practically nothing about them. Most have been seen only a handful of times. Are they rare, or are they simply adept at avoiding us? No one knows; and you will find none of them in this list.

The following list, therefore, is not meant to be in any way a thorough indication of what species may really be endangered in the world's oceans. Instead, it is a compendium of animals that have been given international status—officially and unofficially—as deserving of our special attention.

***IUCN Red List* Classification Codes:**

Ex—Extinct [species not located in the wild during the past fifty years]
E—Endangered [species in danger of extinction]
V—Vulnerable [species likely to become endangered in the near future]

R — Rare [species with small populations that are at risk]

I — Indeterminate [species known to be Endangered, Vulnerable or Rare, but exact category unclear]

K — Insufficiently Known [species suspected of being Endangered, Vulnerable or Rare]

K* — Status under review by International Council for Bird Preservation (ICBP)

T — Threatened [general category; includes species with separate populations in different categories]

CT — Commercially Threatened [species not endangered, but threatened as a commercial resource]

* — not listed by IUCN

US Endangered Species Act Status:
En — Endangered
Th — Threatened
En/Th — Part of population listed as Endangered, part as Threatened

CITES Status:
App. I — Listed on Appendix I of CITES [no trade permitted for primarily commercial purposes]
App. II — Listed on Appendix II of CITES [trade for commercial purposes allowed with appropriate permits]
App. I/II — Part of population on Appendix I, part on Appendix II
App. III — Listed on Appendix III of CITES [equivalent to Appendix II, but listed on the request of a single country rather than by vote]

CORALS, JELLYFISH AND SEA ANEMONES (Phylum Cnidaria)
Note: All stony corals in the orders Scleractina and Coenothecalia, the family Tubiporidae in the order Stolonifera (organ-pipe corals) and the families Milleporidae and Stylasteridae in the order Athecata (fire corals) are listed in CITES Appendix II.

SOFT CORALS
Broad Sea Fan (*Eunicella verrucosa*)
Moderately deep coastal waters from Ireland to the Mediterranean
Threats: local overcollecting for tourist souvenirs
Status: **K**

PRECIOUS CORALS
Precious Corals (20 *Corallium* species)
Mediterranean (*C. rubrum*); Japan and Taiwan, east to the Hawaiian Islands
Threats: overcollecting; silt and pollution (*C. rubrum*)
Status: **CT**

SEA ANEMONES
Ivell's Sea Anemone (*Edwardsia ivellii*)
Known from a single brackish lagoon in Sussex, England; possibly extinct
Threats: development
Status: **EX?**
Starlet Sea Anemone (*Nematostella vectensis*)
Salt marshes of the U.K. and eastern North America
Threats: pollution; drying of pools; human use of marshes
Status: **V**

BLACK CORALS
Black Corals (Family Antipathidae; 150 species)
Tropical and subtropical oceans; a few species in temperate waters
Threats: overcollecting; habitat disturbance (New Zealand)
Status: **CT, App. II**

MOLLUSKS (Phylum Mollusca)

CLAMS (Class Bivalvia)

OYSTERS AND MUSSELS
Black-lipped Pearl Oyster (*Pinctada margaritifera*)
Persian Gulf and Red Sea through warm Indian and Pacific oceans to southern California and Gulf of Mexico; associated with coral reefs
Threats: overcollecting for mother-of-pearl; damage to coral reefs
Status: **CT**
Gold-lipped Pearl Oyster (*Pinctada maxima*)
Burma through Indo-Malaysian region to Japan and northern Australia; associated with coral reefs
Threats: overcollecting for mother-of-pearl; damage to coral reefs
Status: **CT**

VENUS SHELLS
Note: All species of Giant Clams (Tridacnidae) are listed on CITES Appendix II.
Horse's Hoof Clam (*Hippopus hippopus*)
Malay Peninsula to eastern Melanesia
Threats: overcollecting for meat and shells; subsistence harvesting
Status: **I**

China Clam (*H. porcellanus*)
Sulu Archipelago (Philippines) and Indonesia
Threats: overcollecting for meat and shells; subsistence harvesting
Status: **I**
Crocus Clam (*Tridacna crocea*)
Malay Peninsula to Micronesia, Australia and Japan
Threats: overcollecting for meat and shells; subsistence harvesting
Status: **K**
Southern Giant Clam (*T. derasa*)
Philippines, New Guinea, Australia, New Caledonia, Guam, Caroline Islands, Cocos-Keeling
Threats: overcollecting for meat and shells; subsistence harvesting
Status: **V**
Giant Clam (*T. gigas*)
Philippines to Micronesia
Threats: overcollecting for meat and shells; subsistence harvesting
Status: **V**
Small Giant Clam (*T. maxima*)
Red Sea and east Africa, east to Tuamotus, Pitcairn Island, Japan and Australia
Threats: overcollecting for meat and shells; subsistence harvesting
Status: **K**
Scaly Clam (*T. squamosa*)
Red Sea and east and southern Africa, east to Tuamotus, Henderson Island, Japan and Australia
Threats: overcollecting for meat and shells; subsistence harvesting
Status: **I**

SNAILS (Class Gastropoda)

PRIMITIVE SNAILS
Green Snail, Great Green Turban
(*Turbo marmoratus*)
Indo-Pacific, west of Fiji
Threats: overcollecting for shells and
opercula (cat's-eyes)
Status: **CT**

ADVANCED SNAILS
Queen Conch (*Strombus gigas*)
Bermuda through the Caribbean to
Venezuela
Threats: overcollecting for food and
for the ornamental shell trade
Status: **CT** (proposed for CITES
App. II)
Triton's Trumpet (*Charonia tritonis*)
Red Sea, east to Hawaii and Fiji
Threats: overcollecting; possibly,
accumulation of toxic residues from
pesticides
Status: **R**

SEA SLUGS
Zuider Zee Doridella Sea Slug
(*Doridella batava*)
Zuider Zee, Netherlands; possibly
extinct
Threats: closure and drainage of the
Zuider Zee
Status: **K**

SEGMENTED WORMS (Phylum Annelida)

POLYCHAETE WORMS (Class Polychaeta)

PALOLO WORMS
Palolo Worm (*Eunice viridis*)
Pacific
Threats: overfishing; pollution in
harbors
Status: **K**

ARTHROPODS (Phylum Arthropoda) (Class Merostomata)

HORSESHOE CRABS
Asiatic Horseshoe Crabs (*Carcino-scorpius rotundicauda, Tachypleus gigas, T. tridentatus*)
India to the Philippines and Borneo
(*C. rotundicauda, T. gigas*); Japan to
Indonesia (*T. tridentatus*)
Threats: overcollecting for biomedi-
cal research (*T. tridentatus*); pollution
and land reclamation
Status: **K**
American Horseshoe Crab (*Limu-lus polyphemus*)
Atlantic coast of North America
from Nova Scotia to the Yucatan
Threats: overcollecting for eel bait,
animal feed and biomedical research
Status: **K**

CRUSTACEANS (Class Crustacea)

BARNACLES
Armatobalanus nefrens
Monterey to Channel Islands, Cali-
fornia; found only on or embedded
in hydrocorals (*Allopora* and
Errinopora)
Threats: degradation of habitat
Status: **I**
Balanus aquila
California from San Francisco to
San Diego
Threats: vulnerable to alteration of
coastal habitat
Status: **I**

LOBSTERS AND CRABS
Coconut Crab (*Birgus latro*)
Indian and western Pacific oceans
(terrestrial as adults)
Threats: overcollecting for food and
as an aphrodisiac; modification of
coastal habitat (Guam); damage
from radioactive strontium (Bikini,
Eniwetok)
Status: **R**
Rock Lobster (*Jasus edwardsii*)
New Zealand
Threats: overfishing
Status: **CT**
Spiny Lobster (*Panilurus argus*)
North Carolina through Caribbean
to Brazil
Threats: overcollecting by fishermen
and divers
Status: **CT**
Spotted Spiny Lobster (*P. guttatus*)
Caribbean
Threats: overfishing
Status: **CT**
Spiny Lobster (*P. penicillatus*)
Warm waters of the Indian and
western Pacific oceans
Threats: overfishing
Status: **CT**
California Bay Pea Crab (*Parapin-nixa affinis*)
Bays on southern California coast
Threats: extensive modification of
habitat
Status: **K**
American Lobster, Northern Lob-ster (*Homarus americanus*)
Eastern North America from Labra-
dor to Cape Cod, with young lob-
sters ranging south to Virginia
Threats: overfishing
Status: **CT**
European Lobster, Common Lob-ster (*H. gammarus*)
Mediterranean and northeast Atlan-
tic, English Channel, North Sea and
western Baltic
Threats: overfishing
Status: **CT**
**Norway Lobster, Dublin Bay
Prawn, Scampi** (*Nephrops norvegicus*)
European waters of the Mediterra-
nean, Atlantic and North Sea
Threats: overfishing
Status: **CT**

VERTEBRATES (Phylum Chordata)

JAWLESS FISHES (Class Cephalaspidomorphi)

LAMPREYS
Pacific Lamprey (*Lampetra tridentata*)
Japan and Bering Sea to north-central Baja California; ascends rivers to spawn
Threats: one landlocked population endangered; species probably not threatened otherwise
Status: **R**

CARTILAGINOUS FISHES (Class Chondryichthyes)

SHARKS
Whale Shark (*Rhincodon typus*)
Worldwide in temperate and tropical waters
Threats: collision with boats
Status: **I**
Great White Shark (*Carcharodon carcharias*)
Worldwide in temperate and tropical waters
Threats: overfishing
Status: **K**
Basking Shark (*Cetorhinus maximus*)
Nearly worldwide in cool temperate waters
Threats: catching for their oil; collision with boats
Status: **K**

BONY FISHES (Class Osteichthyes)

COELACANTHS
Coelacanth, Gombessa (*Latimeria chalumnae*)
Comoro Islands, Indian Ocean
Threats: though coelacanths are not fished for directly, there is the threat of overcollecting for scientific specimens and for sale of notochordal fluid as a longevity tonic (valued in Japan on the false assumption that fluid from such an ancient fish must have such properties)
Status: **V, App. I**

STURGEONS
Shortnose Sturgeon (*Acipenser brevirostrum*)
New Brunswick to northeast Florida; ascends rivers to spawn
Threats: damming of breeding rivers, cutting off access to spawning sites; pollution; now appears to be recovering
Status: **V, En, App. I**
Atlantic Sturgeon (*A. oxyrhynchus*)
Labrador to Florida and northeast Gulf of Mexico; ascends rivers to spawn
Threats: damming of rivers; commercial fishing (St. Lawrence River)
Status: **V, App. II**
Common Sturgeon (*A. sturio*)
Seas surrounding Europe, including Mediterranean and Black seas; ascends rivers to spawn
Threats: overfishing; pollution of rivers
Status: **E, App. I**

SALMONLIKE FISHES
Delta Smelt (*Hypomesus transpacificus*)
Central California and Japan in brackish and fresh water (Japanese population probably a separate species)
Threats: development and pollution from agricultural runoff in California range
Status: **V**

SALMON AND WHITEFISH
Houting (*Coregonus oxyrhynchus*)
Northern Europe and Asia (fresh and salt water)
Threats: pollution
Status: **E**
*Chinook Salmon, King Salmon (*Oncorhynchus tshawytscha*)
Japan to Bering Sea and south to southern California; ascends rivers to spawn
Threats: pollution and development on breeding rivers; overfishing
Status: **Th (part)**

SILVERSIDES
Key Silverside (*Menidia conchorum*)
Ponded waters of lower Florida Keys
Threats: modification and destruction of habitat
Status: **V**

SEA HORSES AND THEIR RELATIVES
Knysna Sea Horse (*Hippocampus capensis*)
South Africa (Knysna and Kerbooms estuaries; Mossel and Plattenberg bays)
Threats: pollution; development of holiday resorts and lumber industry; oil drilling
Status: **V**

PERCHLIKE FISHES
Totoaba (*Totoaba macdonaldi*)
Northern Gulf of California (Colorado River estuary)
Threats: overfishing; pollution and water reclamation (of the Colorado)
Status: **E, En, App. I**

REPTILES (Class Reptilia)

TURTLES
Loggerhead Turtle (*Caretta caretta*)
Subtropical and, occasionally, tropical coastal waters of the Atlantic, Pacific and Indian oceans
Threats: beachfront development; disturbance and predation at nesting colonies; marine pollution and disturbance from oil and gas drilling and other sources; incidental capture in shrimping and other fishing gear; ingestion of plastics; boat collisions
Status: **V, Th, App. I**
Green Turtle (*Chelonia midas*)
Worldwide in tropical and subtropical waters
Threats: Demand for eggs and meat as human food; degradation of nesting and feeding habitats
Status: **E, En/Th, App. I**

Hawksbill Turtle (*Eretmochelys imbricata*)
Worldwide in clear tropical waters, especially near reefs and rocky areas
Threats: international trade in tortoiseshell; taking of juveniles for sale as stuffed souvenirs; taking for food (localized)
Status: **E, En, App. I**
Kemp's Ridley (*Lepidochelys kempii*)
Gulf of Mexico, ranging north to Long Island; population at perhaps 1 percent of former levels
Threats: marine pollution and disturbance from oil and gas drilling and other sources; incidental capture in shrimping and other fishing gear; ingestion of plastics; disturbance and predation at nesting colonies
Status: **E, En, App. I**
Olive Ridley, Pacific Ridley (*L. olivacea*)
Tropical coastal waters of Pacific, Indian and South Atlantic oceans
Threats: taking for food, leather and oil; egg collecting (Central America)
Status: **E, En/Th, App. I**
Leatherback (*Dermochelys coriacea*)
Almost worldwide; nests almost entirely in the tropics
Threats: taking of eggs and adults for food; ingestion of plastics
Status: **E, En, App. I**

LIZARDS
Galapagos Marine Iguana (*Amblyrhynchus cristatus*)
Galapagos Islands
Threats: local populations vulnerable to potential environmental disturbance
Status: **R, App. II**

CROCODILES
Estuarine, Indo-Pacific or Saltwater Crocodile (*Crocodylus porosus*)
Coastal India and Sri Lanka through Southeast Asia, Indonesia and the Philippines to New Guinea, Australia and Melanesia; may range east to Fiji
Threats: hunting; egg collecting; loss of habitat
Status: **V, En (part), App. I/II**

BIRDS (Class Aves)

PENGUINS
Yellow-eyed Penguin (*Megadyptes antipodes*)
New Zealand and surrounding islands; population 1,200–1,800 pairs
Threats: farm development, human disturbance at nesting sites
Status: **V**
Jackass Penguin (*Spheniscus demersus*)
Namibia and South Africa
Threats: loss of food supply through overfishing; harbor development near breeding sites; oil pollution
Status: **K*, App. II**
Peruvian Penguin (*S. humboldti*)
Peru and Chile
Threats: has been in decline since mid-1800s; El Nino currents in 1980s seriously depleted population
Status: **K*, App. I**
*Galapagos Penguin (*Spheniscus mendiculus*)
Galapagos Islands
Threats: small, localized population vulnerable to habitat disturbance
Status: **En**

TUBE-NOSED SWIMMERS
Amsterdam Albatross (*Diomedea amsterdamensis*)
Amsterdam Island, southern Indian Ocean; population about five pairs
Threats: tiny population size vulnerable to disturbance
Status: **E**
Short-tailed Albatross (*D. albatrus*)
Breeds only on one small island in Japan; ranges over North Pacific; population under 300
Threats: almost exterminated by feather-hunters in nineteenth and early twentieth centuries; volcanic eruptions on Toroshima; now slowly recovering
Status: **R, En, App. I**
Mascarene Black Petrel (*Pterodroma aterrima*)
Reunion, Indian Ocean; known from seven specimens
Threats: unknown
Status: **I**
Black-capped Petrel (*P. hasitata*)
Now breeds only on Hispaniola and Cuba; follows Gulf Stream
Threats: potential disturbance at breeding sites
Status: **R**
Cahow (*P. cahow*)
Bermuda; population thirty-five pairs in early 1980s
Threats: loss of nesting sites
Status: **E, En**
Beck's Petrel (*P. becki*)
Bismarck and Solomon Islands; known from two specimens
Threats: unknown
Status: **I**

Magenta Petrel (*P. magentae*)
Chatham Islands, New Zealand; population 50–100
Threats: small, localized population vulnerable to disturbance
Status: **R**
Gon-gon (*P. feae*)
Cape Verde and Madeira Islands, Atlantic Ocean; population several hundred pairs
Threats: considerable human exploitation
Status: **R**
Freira (*P. madeira*)
Madeira, Atlantic Ocean; population about twenty pairs
Threats: rat predation at breeding sites
Status: **R**
Dark-rumped Petrel (*P. phaeopygia*)
Galapagos and Hawaiian Islands, Pacific Ocean
Threats: predation and habitat destruction at nest sites by introduced mammals
Status: **R**
Cook's Petrel (*P. cooki*)
Islands off New Zealand; population 10,000–50,000 pairs
Threats: predation from introduced animals at nesting colonies
Status: **R**
Chatham Island Petrel (*P. axillaris*)
Rangatira, Chatham Islands, New Zealand; population under 500
Threats: competition for nesting burrows from Broad-billed Prion (*Pachyptila vittata*)
Status: **V**

Defilippe's Petrel (*P. defilippiana*)
Juan Fernandez and Desventuradas Islands, Chile; population several hundred pairs
Threats: predation from feral cats at breeding sites
Status: **V**

Pycroft's Petrel (*P. pycrofti*)
Islands off northeast New Zealand; population under 1,000 pairs
Threats: predation by introduced mammals; environmental damage
Status: **V**

Fiji Petrel (*P. macgillivrayi*)
Gau Island, Fiji; known from three specimens
Threats: potential predation from feral cats
Status: **I**

Black Petrel (*Procellaria parkinsoni*)
Great Barrier and Little Barrier Islands, New Zealand; population under 1,000 pairs
Threats: predation from feral cats
Status: **V**

Westland Black Petrel (*P. westlandica*)
South Island, New Zealand; population 1,000–5,000 pairs
Threats: timber-milling in breeding range
Status: **R**

Pink-footed Shearwater (*Puffinus creatopus*)
Mocha Island and Juan Fernandez Islands, Chile; population 2,000–3,000
Threats: population apparently in decline; disturbance at breeding sites
Status: **V**

Heinroth's Shearwater (*P. heinrothi*)
Bismark and Solomon Islands, Papua New Guinea
Threats: unknown
Status: **I**

Newell's Shearwater (*P. newelli*)
Kauai, Hawaiian Islands
Threats: predation; destruction of breeding colonies by fire; collision of fledgling birds with street lights
Status: **V, Th**

Townsend's Shearwater (*P. auricularis*)
Revillagigedo Islands, Mexico, and Hawaiian Islands
Threats: nest destruction and predation by introduced pigs, cats and mongooses
Status: **E**

Guadalupe Storm-Petrel (*Oceanodroma macrodactyla*)
Guadalupe Islands, Mexico; unrecorded since 1906
Threats: possible predation by feral cats (if the species is not already extinct)
Status: **Ex**

Markham's Storm-Petrel (*O. markhami*)
Waters off western Central and South America
Threats: unknown (breeding grounds not yet discovered)
Status: **I**

Tristram's Storm Petrel (*O. tristrami*)
Southern Izu, Volcano and Leeward Hawaiian Islands, North Pacific
Threats: predation by feral rats and cats on nesting islands (Japan)
Status: **K***

Ringed Storm-Petrel, Hornby's Storm-Petrel (*O. hornbyi*)
Waters off western Central and South America
Threats: unknown (breeding grounds not yet discovered)
Status: **K***

Peruvian Diving-Petrel (*Pelecanoides garnoti*)
Peru and Chile
Threats: introduced predators on breeding islands; egg collecting
Status: **K***

PELICANS AND THEIR RELATIVES

Dalmatian Pelican (*Pelecanus crispus*)
Yugoslavia to western China
Threats: drainage of marshland breeding habitat
Status: **E, App. I**

Spot-billed Pelican (*P. philippensis*)
India east to China, Malaysia and the Philippines
Status: **I**

*Brown Pelican (*P. occidentalis*)
Warm temperate and tropical coasts of North and South America; West Indies; Galapagos Islands
Threats: depleted by DDT spraying; now recovering
Status: **En**

Abbott's Booby (*Sula abbotti*)
Christmas Island, Indian Ocean (extinct elsewhere); population at most 2,000 breeding pairs
Threats: phosphate mining in forested nesting grounds
Status: **E, En**

Rough-faced Shag, New Zealand King Cormorant (*Phalacrocorax carunculatus*)
New Zealand; population under 7,000
Threats: localized breeding range vulnerable to disturbance
Status: **R**

Pygmy Cormorant (*P. pygmaeus*)
Albania to western former USSR
Threats: drainage of wetland habitat
Status: **K***

Galapagos Flightless Cormorant (*Nannopterum harrisi*)
Galapagos Islands; population 800–1,000
Threats: localized, vulnerable population; affected by El Niño currents
Status: **R**

Ascension Frigatebird (*Fregata aquila*)
Boatswainbird Islet off Ascension Island, Atlantic Ocean
Threats: disturbance to breeding site
Status: **R**

Christmas Frigatebird (*F. andrewsi*)
Christmas Island, Indian Ocean; population less than 1,600 pairs
Threats: phosphate mining
Status: **E, En, App. I**

SHOREBIRDS, GULLS AND AUKS

White-eyed Gull (*Larus leucophthalmus*)
Gulf of Aden and Red Sea
Threats: vulnerable to oil spills
Status: **K***

Olrog's Gull (*L. atlanticus*)
Buenos Aires Province, Argentina; population roughly 300
Threats: tourism; fishing traffic; egg collecting; petroleum exploitation
Status: **K***

Audouin's Gull (*L. audouinii*)
Mediterranean Sea; winters to northwest Africa; population roughly 6,000 pairs
Threats: predation of nestlings by Herring Gulls (*L. argentatus*)
Status: **R, En**

Relict Gull (*L. relictus*)
Eastern former USSR and Mongolia
Threats: fluctuating water levels at nesting colonies
Status: **R, En, App. I**

Saunders's Gull (*L. saundersi*)
China and Mongolia
Threats: highly localized breeding range vulnerable to disturbance
Status: **R**

Kerguelen Tern (*Sterna virgata*)
Prince Edward, Crozet and Kerguelen Islands, Indian Ocean
Threats: predation by feral cats
Status: **V**

Black-fronted Tern (*S. albostriata*)
South Island, New Zealand; population 1,000–5,000 pairs
Threats: hydroelectric development at breeding sites
Status: **V**

Damara Tern (*S. balaenarum*)
Namibia and South Africa
Threats: disturbance at breeding colonies
Status: **R**

Chinese Crested Tern (*S. bernsteini*)
Breeding grounds unknown, possibly on islands off Shandong, China; China to Thailand and Philippines
Threats: unknown
Status: **I**

***Roseate Tern** (*Sterna dougallii*)
Scattered populations almost worldwide in tropical and temperate latitudes
Threats: egg collecting; competition for nesting sites with other seabirds
Status: **En/Th**

***Least Tern** (*S. antillarum*)
Breeds on both coasts of North America (California to Mexico on Pacific, Maine to Florida on Atlantic); also on inland waterways
Threats: development, pollution and human use of nesting beaches; predation by foxes (California)
Status: **En**

Japanese Murrelet (*Synthliboramphus wumizusume*)
Izu Islands, Japan; population estimated at 1,650
Threats: disturbance from sport fishing near nesting sites
Status: **V**

MAMMALS (Class Mammalia)

WHALES, PORPOISES AND DOLPHINS

Note: All cetaceans are listed on Appendix II of CITES, except those listed below as on Appendix I.

Susu, Ganges River Dolphin (*Platanista gangentica*)
Ganges, Brahmaputra, Karnaphuli and Meghna river systems of India, Bangladesh, Nepal and Bhutan (freshwater only)
Threats: extensive habitat damage, especially from dam construction; direct and incidental catching; pollution; boat traffic
Status: **V, App. I**

Indus River Dolphin (*P. minor*)
Indus River system, Pakistan (freshwater only); population approximately 500
Threats: illegal catching for meat and oil; habitat destruction
Status: **E, En, App. I**

Baiji, Yangtze River Dolphin (*Lipotes vexillifer*)
Changjiang (Yangtze) River, China (freshwater only); population approximately 300
Threats: incidental catching; collision with boats; use of explosives for construction and (illegally) for fishing; extensive habitat damage; possible food shortage
Status: **E, App. I**

Franciscana, La Plata Dolphin (*Pontoporia blainvillei*)
Coastal central Atlantic from Espiritu Santo, Brazil, to Peninsula Valdez, Argentina
Threats: large incidental take in gill nets by Uruguayan shark fishery
Status: **K**

Boto, Amazon River Dolphin (*Inia geoffrensis*)
Orinoco and Amazon basins (freshwater only)
Threats: hydroelectric dam construction; incidental catching; deforestation; pollution
Status: **V**

Beluga, White Whale (*Delphinapterus leucas*)
Arctic and subarctic seas
Threats: pollution; hunting
Status: **K**

Narwhal (*Monodon monoceros*)
High Arctic seas
Threats: subsistence hunting; ivory trade; pollution
Status: **K**

Harbor Porpoise (*Phocoena phocoena*)
Shallow, cold temperate and subarctic waters of the Northern Hemisphere
Threats: incidental taking in gill nets; hunting (especially in western Greenland)
Status: **K**

Vaquita (*P. sinus*)
Northern Gulf of California, Mexico; population perhaps in low hundreds
Threats: incidental taking in gill nets; habitat destruction
Status: **E, En, App. I**

***Finless Porpoise** (*Neophocaena phocaenoides*)
Warm rivers and coastal waters from the Persian Gulf to Indonesia and Japan
Threats: habitat destruction; incidental and direct taking
Status: **App. I**

*Indo-Pacific Humpback Dolphin (*Sousa chinensis*)
Coastal and inshore waters of the Indian and western Pacific oceans
Threats: incidental taking; damage to inshore habitats
Status: **App. I**

*Atlantic Humpback Dolphin (*S. teuszii*)
West Africa
Threats: incidental taking; potential overfishing of food supply; potential damage to mangrove habitat
Status: **App. I**

*Tucuxi (*Sotalia fluviatilis*)
Atlantic coast from Panama to Parana, Brazil (ascends rivers); Amazon river drainage
Threats: construction of hydroelectric dams; incidental taking in nets and traps
Status: **App. I**

Commerson's Dolphin (*Cephalorhynchus commersonii*)
Southern South America, Falklands (South Atlantic), Kerguelen (Indian Ocean)
Threats: illegal harpooning for crab bait; some incidental taking
Status: **K**

Black Dolphin (*C. eutropia*)
Chile
Threats: illegal harpooning for crab bait
Status: **K**

Heaviside's Dolphin (*C. heavisidii*)
Southern Africa
Threats: incidental taking in nets
Status: **K**

Hector's Dolphin (*C. hectori*)
New Zealand; population approximately 3,000–4,000
Threats: entanglement in gill nets takes high proportion of population
Status: **V**

Irrawaddy Dolphin (*Orcaella brevirostris*)
Bay of Bengal to northern Australia (freshwater, some coastal habitats)
Threats: direct and indirect catching; habitat destruction
Status: **K**

*Baird's Beaked Whale (*Berardius bairdii*)
North Pacific, Sea of Japan and Sea of Okhotsk
Threats: Japanese commercial whaling
Status: **App. I**

*Arnoux's Beaked Whale (*B. arnuxii*)
Antarctic and subantarctic seas
Threats: potential threat from increased fishing in the Southern Ocean
Status: **App. I**

Northern Bottlenose Whale (*Hyperoodon ampullatus*)
North Atlantic and surrounding seas
Threats: none at present, but species has not recovered from former commercial whaling pressure (to 1973)
Status: **V, App. I**

*Southern Bottlenose Whale (*H. planifrons*)
Southern Ocean north to about 30°S
Threats: incidental taking in drift nets
Status: **App. I**

Note: There may be a third species of *Hyperoodon*, as yet undescribed, in the tropical Pacific; if so, it will automatically be covered under CITES Appendix I, as the listing is for the entire genus.

*Sperm Whale (*Physeter macrocephalus*)
All oceans
Threats: commercial whaling (now suspended); incidental taking
Status: **En, App. I**

Bowhead Whale (*Balaena mysticetus*)
Arctic and subarctic waters; now in numbers (approximately 7,800) only in Bering, Chuchki and Beaufort seas; a few hundred elsewhere
Threats: depleted by commercial whaling, now suspended; potential industrial damage in Alaska; aboriginal subsistence hunting
Status: **V, En, App. I**

Northern Right Whale (*Eubalaena glacialis*)
North Atlantic and North Pacific oceans; only a few hundred remain
Threats: almost wiped out by commercial whaling, ended in 1920s; has failed to recover; incidental taking, collision with ships, habitat degradation; possible future threats from industrial development
Status: **E, En, App. I**

Southern Right Whale (*E. australis*)
Southern oceans from about 20° to 50°S; population at least 1,500
Threats: severely depleted by commercial whaling, now suspended; incidental taking, collision with ships, habitat degradation
Status: **V, En, App. I**

*Pygmy Right Whale (*Caperea marginata*)
Temperate waters of the Southern Hemisphere between 31° and 52°S
Threats: possibly incidental taking in nets
Status: **App. I**

*Gray Whale (*Eschrichtius robustus*)
North Pacific; formerly North Atlantic
Threats: severely depleted by commercial whaling in past, but eastern Pacific population has recovered; incidental take in gill nets; possible threat from human visitor pressure in calving lagoons
Status: **En, App. I**

*Minke Whale (*Balaenoptera acutorostrata*)
All oceans
Threats: some stocks depleted by commercial whaling, now officially suspended though some subsistence whaling in Greenland and Japan continues to take roughly 300 minkes a year for "scientific research"; there is strong pressure to reopen commercial taking of minkes
Status: **App. I/II**

*Sei Whale (*B. borealis*)
Most oceans and seas
Threats: depleted by commercial whaling, now carried on only near Iceland
Status: **En, App. I**

*Bryde's Whale (*B. edeni*)
Tropical and warm temperate waters worldwide
Threats: commercial whaling (now suspended); depletion of food-fish species from overfishing
Status: **App. I**

Blue Whale (*B. musculus*)
Worldwide; population in low thousands
Threats: almost exterminated by commercial whaling (legally ended 1964, but some has occurred since)
Status: **E, En, App. I**
Fin Whale (*B. physalus*)
Worldwide
Threats: greatly reduced by commercial whaling (ended 1975 except for North Atlantic); subsistence whaling (Greenland); heavy metal poisoning of food supply (Mediterranean)
Status: **V, En, App. I**
Humpback Whale (*Megaptera novaeangliae*)
Worldwide; population approximately 25,000
Threats: greatly reduced by commercial whaling; vulnerable to poisoning during "red tides"
Status: **V, En, App. I**

CARNIVORES
WEASELS
Marine Otter, Chingungo (*Lutra felina*)
Coasts of Peru and Chile
Threats: hunting for fur; persecution by fishermen
Status: **V, App. I**
*Sea Otter (*Enhydra lutris*) Coastal North Pacific from Japan to Alaska and south to Baja California
Threats: almost exterminated through hunting for fur, now ended; contamination from oil spills; entanglement in gill nets
Status: **Th(part), App. I/II (all other otters on App. II)**

SEALS AND SEA LIONS
*Northern Sea Lion, Steller's Sea Lion (*Eumetopias jubatus*)
Northern Japan to Alaska and California
Threats: competition for food with commercial fisheries; entanglement in fishing gear
Status: **Th**
Guadalupe Fur Seal (*Arctocephalus townsendi*)
Guadalupe Island, Mexico; population 500–1,000
Threats: almost exterminated by sealers in the nineteenth century; vulnerable to disturbance on breeding grounds
Status: **V, Th, App. I**
Juan Fernandez Fur Seal (*A. philippii*)
Juan Fernandez and San Felix Islands, Chile; population probably under 2,000
Threats: almost exterminated by sealers in eighteenth and nineteenth centuries
Status: **V, App. II**
Note: All other fur seals in the genus *Arctocephalus* are listed on Appendix II of CITES.
*Walrus (*Odobenus rosmarus*)
Coasts of Arctic Ocean and nearby seas
Threats: poaching for ivory; subsistence hunting
Status: **App. III**

Mediterranean Monk Seal (*Monachus monachus*)
Mediterranean and Black seas and adjacent Atlantic waters off North Africa; population 500–1,000
Threats: pollution; persecution by fishermen
Status: **E, En, App. I**
Hawaiian Monk Seal (*M. schauinslandi*)
Leeward Chain, Hawaiian Islands
Threats: disturbance on breeding islands
Status: **E, En, App. I**
Caribbean Monk Seal, West Indian Monk Seal (*M. tropicalis*)
Bahamas and Yucatan through Caribbean Sea; last recorded 1952
Threats: formerly hunted for oil
Status: **Ex?, En, App. I**
*Northern Elephant Seal (*Mirounga angustirostris*)
California and Baja California, breeding on offshore islands
Threats: almost exterminated by sealers in nineteenth century, but has recovered well; possibly out of danger
Status: **App. II**
*Southern Elephant Seal (*M. leonina*)
Circumpolar in subantarctic seas
Threats: almost exterminated by sealing in the nineteenth century (ended 1964); depletion of food supply through overfishing
Status: **App. II**

SIRENIANS
Dugong (*Dugong dugon*)
Warm waters of Indian and western Pacific oceans; extinct in Mediterranean
Threats: entanglement in nylon fishing nets; overhunting for meat, oil and incisor teeth (used as amulets in southeast Asia)
Status: **V, En, App. I/II**
Steller's Sea Cow (*Hydrodamalis gigas*)
Bering Sea; probably extinct since eighteenth century, though occasionally still reported
Threats: exterminated by overhunting in eighteenth century
Status: **Ex**
Amazonian Manatee (*Trichechus inunguis*)
Amazon basin and coastal waters of Brazil
Threats: overhunting for oil, meat and hides
Status: **V, En, App. I**
West Indian Manatee (*T. manatus*)
Southern United States through Caribbean to South America
Threats: hunting, pollution; entanglement in fishing gear; collision with power boats
Status: **V, En, App. I**
West African Manatee (*T. senegalensis*)
Coastal waters and rivers of west Africa from Senegal to Angola
Threats: hunting; pollution; entanglement in fishing gear
Status: **V, Th, App. II**

MARINE ENVIRONMENTAL ORGANIZATIONS

RONALD ORENSTEIN

One of the best ways you can help in the fight to save the world's oceans is by supporting one of the many environmental organizations devoted to marine conservation. The following list includes most, if not all, of the major organizations and a good many smaller ones dedicated to such causes as the preservation of whales and dolphins. If any of them sound interesting to you, be sure to write or call them for information before you write a check. Ask how large they are, what projects they are engaged in, how much of their budget goes to ocean projects, and whether or not they provide their members or donors with newsletters or magazines. If you live near one of them, and want to help in a direct way, ask if they welcome volunteers. You may find yourself doing everything from testing polluted water to saving a beached whale—not to mention the less glamorous but vitally necessary jobs of mailing, letter-writing or just helping in the office. It's the best way to do your part in saving the oceans.

Addresses marked with an asterisk (*) are the head offices of organizations with local branches in many countries. You can write them for information on branches in your area.

Australia

Australian Conservation Foundation
340 Gore Street
Fitzroy, VIC 3065
Australia

Australian Whale Conservation
Society
P.O. Box 238
North Quay, QLD 4002
Australia

Fund for Animals
P.O. Box 126
Terry Hills, NSW 2084
Australia

International Cetacean Education
Research Centre
P.O. Box 110
Nambucca, NSW 2448
Australia

Port Phillip Bay Dolphin Research
Project
P.O. Box 721
Hawthorne, VIC 3122
Australia

Project Jonah
340 Gore Street
Fitzroy, VIC 3065
Australia

Sea Shepherd Conservation Society
P.O. Box 195
Paddington, NSW 2021
Australia

Whale Rescue Centre
Room 16, 37 Swanson St.
Melbourne, VIC 3000
Australia

Wildwatch Inc.
P.O. Box 313
Eastwood, SA 5063
Australia

Brazil

International Wildlife Coalition—
Brasil
P.O. Box 5087
Florianópolis, SC
Brasil 88041

Canada

International Wildlife Coalition—
Canada
P.O. Box 461
Port Credit Postal Station
Mississauga, Ontario
Canada L5G 4M1

Ocean Voice
2883 Otterson Avenue
Ottawa, Ontario
Canada K1V 7B2

Orcalab
P.O. Box 258
Alert Bay, British Columbia
Canada V0N 1A0

Zoocheck Canada
5334 Yonge Street
Toronto, Ontario Canada M2N 6M2

Chile

CODEFF (Comite Nacéional Pro
Defensa de la Fauna y Flora)
Casilla 3675
Santiago
Chile

Union de los Amigos de los
Animales
Godofredo Stutzin
Casilla 3675
Santiago
Chile

France

Fondation Cousteau
25, avenue de Wagram
75017 Paris
France

Japan

Nature Conservation Society of
Japan (NACS-J)
(Nihon Shizen Hogo Kyōkai)
Toranomon Denki Bldg.
2-8-1 Toranomon
Minato-ku, Tokyo 105
Japan

Netherlands

*Greenpeace International
Keizersgracht 176
1016 DW
Amsterdam
Netherlands

New Zealand

Project Interlock
Wade and Jane Doak
P.O. Box 20
Whangerei
New Zealand

Project Jonah
P.O. Box 31 357
Milford, Auckland
New Zealand

South Africa

Dolphin Action and Protection
Group
P.O. Box 227
Fish Hoek 7975
South Africa

Seal Action Group
P.O. Box 15877
Viseberg 8018
South Africa

Switzerland

*World Fund for Nature (WWF)
International
CH 1196
Gland
Switzerland

United Kingdom

*Environmental Investigation
Agency
208/209 Upper St.
London N1 1Rl
United Kingdom

*Friends of the Earth
26-28 Underwood St.
London N1 7JQ
United Kingdom

International Dolphin Watch
Parklands, North Fermby
Humberside HU14 3ET
United Kingdom

*International Fund for Animal
Welfare
35 Boundary Road
St. John's Wood
London NW8 0JE
United Kingdom

Marine Conservation Society
4 Gloucester Road
Ross-on-Wye
Hertfordshire HR9 5BV
United Kingdom

Whale and Dolphin Conservation
Society
20 West Lea Road
Bath BA1 3RL
Avon
United Kingdom

*World Society for the Protection
of Animals
106 Jermyn Street
London SW1 6EE
United Kingdom

USA

American Cetacean Society
P.O. Box 2639
San Pedro, CA
USA 90731

Center for Coastal Studies
P.O. Box 826
Provincetown, MA
USA 02657

Center for Marine Conservation
1725 DeSales St. NW, Suite 500
Washington, DC
USA 20036

Cetacean Society International
P.O. Box 9145
190 Stillwood Drive
Wethersfield, CT
USA 06109

Clean Water Action
1320 18th St. NW
Washington, DC
USA 20036

The Cousteau Society, Inc.
930 W. 12th St.
Norfolk, VA
USA 23517

Defenders of Wildlife
1244 19th St. NW
Washington, DC
USA 20036

The Dolphin Network
3220 Sacramento St.
San Francisco, CA
USA 94115

Dolphin Project, Inc.
P.O. Box 224
Coconut Grove, FL
USA 33233

Dolphin Research Centre
P.O. Box 2875
Marathon Shores, FL
USA 33052

Earth Island Institute
300 Broadway, Suite 28
San Francisco, CA 94133

Earthtrust
2500 Pali Highway
Honolulu, HI
USA 96817

Friends of the Sea Otter
P.O. Box 221220
Carmel, CA
USA 93922

Friends of Whales
10830 SW 85th Court
Gainesville, FL
USA 32608

Global Cetacean Coalition
2100 L Street NW
Washington, DC
USA 20037

Human/Dolphin Foundation
33307 Decker School Road
Malibu, CA
USA 90625-9608

Humane Society of the United
States
2100 L St. NW
Washington, DC
USA 20037

International Fund for Animal
Welfare
411 Main Street
Yarmouth Port, MA
USA 02675

International Marinelife Alliance
94 Station Street, Suite 645
Hingham, MA
USA 02043

*International Wildlife Coalition
(Whale Adoption Project)
Holly Park
634 North Falmouth Highway
North Falmouth, MA
USA 02556

Lifeforce
P.O. Box 210354
San Francisco, CA
USA 94121

Marine Mammal Stranding Center
Box 753
Brigantine, NJ
USA 08203

The Monitor Consortium
1506 19th St. NW
Washington, DC
USA 20036

North American Native Fishes
Association
123 West Mt. Airy Ave.
Philadelphia, PA
USA 19119

The Oceanic Society
1596 16th St. NW
Washington, DC
USA 20036

Pacific Whale Foundation
101 N. Kihei Rd.
Kihei, HI
USA 96753

Save the Manatee Club
500 North Maitland Avenue
Suite 210
Maitland, FL
USA 32751

Save the Whales, Inc.
1426 Main St., Unit E
P.O. Box 2397
Venice, CA
USA 90291

Sea Shepherd Conservation Society
P.O. Box 7000-S
Redondo Beach, CA
USA 90277

The Sea Turtle Center
P.O. Box 634
Nevada City, CA
USA 95959

University of the Sea
A Volunteer Research Organization
Old College, 401 West Second
Reno, Nevada 89503

West Quoddy Biological Research
Station
P.O. Box 9
Lubec, ME
USA 04625

Whale Center
3933 Piedmont Avenue #2
Oakland, CA
USA 94611

Whale and Dolphin Conservation
Society USA
191 Weston Rd.
Lincoln, MA
USA 01773

World Society for the Protection of
Animals
29 Perkins St.
P.O. Box 190
Boston, MA
USA 02130

QUICK REFERENCE LIST ON THE OCEANS AND SEAS

• Seawater covers over two-thirds of the Earth. Geographers and mapmakers identify four major bodies of water: the Pacific, Atlantic, Indian and Arctic oceans. The Southern Ocean is not usually considered a separate ocean because it is not well defined by surrounding land. The **largest ocean** is the Pacific Ocean at 64,186,300 square miles (166 million km²), followed by the Atlantic Ocean at 33,420,000 square miles (87 million km²), the Indian Ocean at 28,350,500 square miles (73 million km²) and the Arctic Ocean at 5,105,700 square miles (13 million km²).

• Seas are partially enclosed by land, such as the Mediterranean Sea, or are specific areas of relatively open ocean, such as the South China Sea and the Arabian Sea. The **largest sea** is the South China Sea, and the **largest bay** is Hudson Bay.

• Seawater is about 3 percent sodium chloride, or common salt. Salinity is measured as the number of parts of salt in one thousand parts of seawater (0/00). The average salinity of ocean water is 35/00. The **saltiest water** (42/00) is found in the Red Sea.

• Currents circulate water throughout the oceans, moving warm water from the Equator and cold water from the Arctic and Antarctic. They move clockwise in the Northern Hemisphere and counterclockwise in the Southern Hemisphere. The Gulf Stream in the Atlantic, the Kuroshio in the Pacific, and the Antarctic Circumpolar Current are three of the primary ocean currents. At its peak, the Gulf Stream moves at a rate of up to 140 miles (220 km) per day.

• Tides cause sea levels to rise and fall twice a day on average, and are produced by the gravitational pull of the sun and the moon on the waters of the ocean. The **highest tides** in the world occur in the Bay of Fundy in Canada, where the difference between high and low tide can exceed fifty feet (15 m) at the head of the bay.

• The **deepest areas** of the ocean are located in the Pacific. They are the Mariana Trench, east of the Mariana Islands, at 38,635 feet (11,708 m), and the Tonga Trench, south-southwest of Samoa, which averages almost 33,000 feet (11,000 m) in depth.

• The Atlantic Ocean floor grows by 1.5 inches (4 cm) every year. This occurs where tectonic plates spread and magma rises, forming underwater mountain ranges. The Mid-Atlantic Ridge is the **largest mountain range** in the world. It is over 7,000 miles (11,265 km) long and up to 2.5 miles (4 km) high.

• Subduction zones are areas where tectonic plates collide, and one plate is pushed under the other. The **largest subduction zone** is located along the west coast of South America.

• The **largest coral reef system** in the world is the Great Barrier Reef off the northeast coast of Australia.

• The **largest ocean animal** is the blue whale (*Balaenoptera musculus*), which can weigh up to 170 tons.

GLOSSARY

Abyss, abyssal The part, or concerning the part, of the ocean that lies below 13,100 feet (4,000 m).

Abyssal plain The flat floor of the deep ocean.

Algae Primitive plants, ranging from unicellular organisms to large seaweeds, that form the base of complex oceanic food webs. They are becoming more economically important as a human food source, particularly in Asia.

Asthenosphere The semifluid layer of the Earth lying beneath the lithosphere.

Atoll A circular island of coral reef enclosing a lagoon.

Bacteria One-celled organisms that have no distinct nuclei. Those that break down organic material, including industrial waste and sewage sludge, have helped offset damage to the seas.

Barrier reef A reef running parallel to land and separated from it by a lagoon or channel.

Bathyl zone The ocean zone from the edge of the continental shelf to where water temperatures do not exceed 4°C.

Bathypelagic zone Marine biological zone between 3,300 and 13,100 feet (1,000 and 4,000 m), where no light penetrates.

Bioluminescence The light produced by, or the emission of light from, living organisms. In the sea, photophores—light-producing organs—may act as lures to attract prey, as signals to would-be mates or as a way to confuse a predator.

Brackish water A mixture of salt and fresh water found in estuaries and tidal marshes.

Continental drift theory The theory proposed by Alfred Wegener that the continents were once part of a supercontinent, which broke apart. Over time, the continents have moved away from one another to their present locations.

Continental rise The part of the seabed that rises from the abyssal plain to the continental slope.

Continental shelf The shallow part of the seabed stretching from the shoreline to the continental slope.

Continental slope The steeply sloping part of the seabed between the continental shelf and the continental rise.

Coral Small marine organisms that are solitary or colonial. After death, the calcium-containing skeletons of those that live in colonies in tropical and subtropical seas, along with the algae that live with them, accumulate to form reefs. Those that live in colder and deeper waters are solitary.

Crust The outermost layer of the Earth, which is from ten to twenty-five miles (16 to 40 km) thick. The thinnest part of the crust lies beneath the ocean.

Crustaceans Mainly aquatic, typically hard-shelled arthropods, such as shrimps, crabs, lobsters and barnacles.

DDT A toxic synthetic organic chemical used as a pesticide. It was banned in the industrialized countries in the late 1970s but is still in use in some Third World countries.

Deep scattering layers Sound-reflecting layers in the ocean that can be detected by echo-sounding equipment. The vertical movement of the layers up toward the surface during the day and down at night corresponds to the movement of certain marine organisms.

Dredging The removal of sediment from estuaries to form harbors, or from natural harbors, rivers and canals to deepen them for navigation.

Drift net A type of plastic gill net that is suspended vertically from the surface by floats. Drift nets, which can be joined together and laid out over long distances, trap marine mammals, seabirds and turtles, as well as fish.

Earthquake A sudden movement of a part of the Earth's surface, caused by volcanic activity or faulting.

Echinoderms Marine invertebrates, including starfish, sea urchins, feather stars, sea cucumbers and brittle stars, characterized by fivefold symmetry, a calcareous skeleton and a water-vascular system used for respiration, feeding or movement

Echolocation The ability to project sound through water and locate an object by the echo reflected back. Some types of whales, sea lions, seals and walrus use echolocation.

Echo sounding A technique used by scientists to detect undersea objects or to map ocean terrain by projecting sound through water and registering the echo reflected back.

Epipelagic zone The sunlit zone of the ocean, extending from the surface to a depth of about 650 feet (200 m).

Estuary A river mouth, inlet or bay where fresh and salt water are mixed by tidal water movement.

Eutrophication A process that changes a body of water from its natural state to one rich in dissolved nutrients, such as nitrogen and phosphorus. These nutrients, in turn, promote rapid plant growth, particularly of algae. When the bottom layer of algae dies, it forms a decomposing mass that deoxygenates the water, making it unfit for other life.

Extinction The disappearance of an entire species.

Fault A geological term referring to a break or fracture zone in the Earth's crust.

Fish Cold-blooded marine animals that breathe by means of gills.

Food chain In a food chain, the food energy of one kind of organism is consumed by another kind of organism. Each organism in the sequence is dependent upon the population it feeds on and its environment.

Fresh water Water that is drinkable, containing very little salt.

Greenhouse effect The term used to describe a rise in mean temperatures around the world, which is attributed to an increase in the level of carbon dioxide in the atmosphere over the past 200 years.

Hadal zone Marine biological zone of the ocean lying below 20,000 feet (6,000 m).

Hazardous wastes Wastes that present an immediate or long-term human health risk or that pose a risk to the environment.

Hydrothermal vent A vent of heated, mineral-rich water, usually occurring along the edges of crustal plates.

Intertidal zone. *See* Littoral zone.

Lagoon An area of water separated from the ocean by a coral reef, sandbar or barrier island.

Lithosphere The crust and upper mantle of the Earth.

Littoral zone The coastal area that lies between the low-tide mark and the high-tide mark. Also called the intertidal zone.

Mammal A warm-blooded, air-breathing animal whose young are fed with milk from the female's mammary glands. Sea mammals include seals, walruses and whales.

Mantle Geologically, the zone extending from below the Earth's crust to its core. Biologically, the membrane that covers the soft body of a mollusk.

Mesopelagic zone Marine biological zone between 650 and 3,300 feet (200 and 1,000 m), where little light penetrates. Also called the twilight zone.

Migration The regular journeys of animals to and from breeding and feeding areas.

Mollusk An animal with a soft body covered by a mantle and often a hard shell. Mollusks include scallops, snails, clams, octopuses and squid.

PCBs (*polychlorinated biphenyls*) Long-lived toxic chemicals used in electrical transformers and condensers in industrialized countries until the late 1970s. (They are still used in much of the developing world.) PCBs have found their way into the ocean food chain as a result of improper disposal. High concentrations are fatal, while low-level contamination can interfere with reproduction, affect the immune system and retard the growth of marine life.

Pelagic Of the open sea, excluding the bottom and the shore.

Photosynthesis The process by which plants and some chlorophyll-containing organisms change water and carbon dioxide into carbohydrates, using light from the sun as the source of energy and with the aid of chlorophyll. Oxygen is released during the process.

Phytoplankton. *See* Plankton.

Plankton Tiny plant and animal life found floating in the ocean. The phytoplankton, which are photosynthesizing organisms, form the base of the oceanic food chain. Recent studies have shown that the thinning of the atmospheric ozone layer over Antarctica and the resulting rise in ultraviolet radiation has caused a reduction in the production of phytoplankton. Zooplankton are non-photosynthesizing organisms.

Plate tectonics A geological theory concerning the movement of huge blocks or plates of the lithosphere.

Purse seine A circular fishing net which can be drawn tightly around schools of pelagic fish like a bag. Old-fashioned purse seines also trap dolphins. These nets have been redesigned to allow dolphins accidentally caught in them to escape.

Red tide Seawater covered by masses of certain species of dinoflagellates (phytoplankton), containing toxins which are poisonous to many types of marine life and to humans who eat infected clams and mussels.

Rift valley A trough caused by the collapse of a section of the Earth's crust.

Seawater Salt water from the ocean, comprising approximately 97 percent of all the water on Earth.

Sediment Solid organic and inorganic material originating on land and in the sea that settles to the bottom.

Seismology The study of earthquakes and man-made shock waves, such as those produced by nuclear explosions.

Sewage sludge Organic and inorganic matter discharged by sewage treatment plants into the sea. Sludge from industrialized areas often contains heavy metals such as mercury, cadmium and lead.

Sounding Determining depth, especially by lowering a weighted line to the bottom.

Sponges Multicellular, filter-feeding marine animals that have a porous structure.

Submersibles Small battery-powered vessels that can remain submerged for a long period of time.

Sunlit zone. *See* Epipelagic zone.

Tide The regular rise and fall of sea level due to the gravitational pull of the sun and moon on the waters of the ocean.

Toxic wastes Substances that cause death or serious injury to humans or animals.

Twilight zone. *See* Mesopelagic zone.

Volcano An oceanic or terrestrial hill or mountain formed around a vent in the Earth's crust through which molten or hot rock and steam are ejected.

Zooplankton. *See* Plankton.

ABOUT THE CONTRIBUTORS

General Editor

Joseph MacInnis

Early in his career Dr. MacInnis provided medical support for some of the deepest and longest manned dives in history. He was the first man to dive and film beneath the North Pole, and later designed the world's first polar dive station, a four-man capsule built beneath the ice 600 miles (1,000 km) north of the Arctic Ocean. Since 1970, he has turned his attention to broader issues that affect the oceans, such as pollution, energy and resources.

Between 1970 and 1983, Dr. MacInnis led fifteen scientific expeditions into the Arctic, becoming the first person to film harp seals and bowhead whales in their underwater environment. In 1980 he led the search team that discovered the *Breadalbane*, sunk in 1853 and the world's northernmost shipwreck. Recently, he has turned his attention to human performance in the deep ocean. In 1987, he explored the *Titanic*, and in 1989, he became the first western scientist to dive three miles (5 km) into the Atlantic with the Russians in their new extreme-depth submersibles.

To increase public awareness of the oceans, Dr. MacInnis has hosted a television series and six films, and has written several books, as well as numerous scientific papers and popular articles for such publications as *National Geographic* and *Scientific American*. His work has earned him a number of distinctions, including three honorary doctorates, the Queen's Anniversary Medal and his country's highest honor, the Order of Canada.

Contributors

Michael Donoghue

Michael Donoghue is the Principal Conservation Officer (Marine Mammals) with the New Zealand Department of Conservation. He has been a scientific advisor to his country's delegation at the International Whaling Commission, and has represented Greenpeace and the Antarctic and South Ocean Coalitions in lobbying to conserve marine life. He is also involved in work to save New Zealand's unique Hector's dolphin and is the co-author of a book called *Save the Dolphins*.

Sylvia Earle

Dr. Earle has logged over five thousand hours underwater as a marine botanist and shares a solo depth record of 3,002 feet (915 m) with only three other people. Her extensive field experience includes leading more than fifty expeditions, using conventional and saturation diving techniques, as well as various submersibles and one-person diving systems. She heads Deep Ocean Engineering, Inc., which designs, develops, manufactures and operates ocean equipment. The recipient of numerous honors and awards, Dr. Earle has written more than seventy publications concerning marine science and technology, has participated in numerous television productions and has delivered lectures in more than fifty countries.

Hillary Hauser

Like our other contributors, Hillary Hauser characterizes herself as a person who loves the sea. In her career as a writer, photographer and diver, she has written for numerous magazines, including *National Geographic, Oceans, Geo* (Germany), *Ocean Science News* and *Esquire*, and has contributed to several anthologies. Among her published books are *Women in Sports: Scuba Diving, The Living World of the Reef* and *Call to Adventure*. In 1989, she was elected into the Explorers Club, an exclusive New York-based organization dedicated to scientific exploration.

John Lythgoe

Dr. Lythgoe is Senior Research Fellow at Bristol University in Bristol, England. He is well known in the scientific community for his work on the ecology of color vision, with special reference to fish. A regular contributor to scientific journals, he is also the author of two books: *The Ecology of Vision* and *Fishes of the Sea*, a photographic identification guide.

A small abandoned cabin over-looks Northumberland Strait between Nova Scotia and Prince Edward Island, Canada.

STEPHEN SCOTT PATTERSON

Ronald Orenstein

Dr. Orenstein is a zoologist and lawyer. He serves as project director for the International Wildlife Coalition and as chairman of the Scientific Advisory Council of Zoocheck Canada. He is the general editor of *Elephants: The Deciding Decade*.

T. R. Parsons

Dr. Parsons is a professor of oceanography at the University of British Columbia in Vancouver. He has written over 150 scientific papers and several textbooks, and is also on the editorial board of five oceanographic magazines.

Peter A. Rona

Dr. Rona is senior research geophysicist with the National Oceanic and Atmospheric Administration and adjunct professor at the University of Miami. A pioneer in exploration of the abyss, he is credited with many discoveries, including the discovery of the first hot springs in the Atlantic. He has led numerous expeditions with surface ships and submersibles to the Atlantic, Pacific and Indian oceans, has written over 150 scientific articles and several books, and lectures internationally.

Anatoly Sagalevitch

A marine engineer and pilot, Dr. Sagalevitch was responsible for the design and construction of the two Russian research submersibles, *Mir 1* and *Mir 2*. He is head of the Manned Submersibles Laboratory of the P.P. Shirshov Institute in Moscow.

Marie Tharp

A well-known geologist and cartographer, Marie Tharp has been an oceanographer with the U.S. Naval Oceanographic Office and a Senior Staff Associate in Geological Sciences at the Lamont-Doherty Geological Observatory. Many of the maps she produced in collaboration with Bruce Heezen continue to be reproduced in publications throughout the world. She has contributed to numerous scientific magazines, including *Science* and *Natural History*, and has written chapters for a number of textbooks. Now retired, she is the president of a map distribution business.

INDEX